INTERPRETERS WITH LEWIS AND CLARK

The Story of Sacagawea and Toussaint Charbonneau

Interpreters with Lewis and Clark

The Story of Sacagawea and Toussaint Charbonneau

W. Dale Nelson

University of North Texas Press
Denton, Texas

The paper in this book meets the minimum requirements of the American National Standard for Permanence of Paper for Printed Library Materials,
Z39.48.1984

Permissions
University of North Texas Press
PO Box 311336
Denton, TX 76203-1336
940-565-2142

Library of Congress Cataloging-in-Publication Data

Nelson, W. Dale.
  Interpreters with Lewis and Clark : the story of Sacagawea and
Toussaint Charbonneau / W. Dale Nelson.— 1st ed.
    p. cm.
Includes bibliographical references and index.
  ISBN 1-57441-165-9 (alk. paper)
  1. Sacagawea. 2. Sacagawea—Family. 3. Charbonneau, Toussaint, ca. 1758-ca.
1839. 4. Charbonneau, Jean-Baptiste, 1805-1866. 5. Shoshoni women—West
(U.S.)—Biography. 6. Pioneers—West (U.S.)—Biography. 7. Indian interpret-
ers—West (U.S.)—Biography. 8. Lewis and Clark Expedition (1804-1806)
9. West (U.S.)—Discovery and exploration. 10. Frontier and pioneer life—
West (U.S.) I. Title.
F592.7.S123 N45 2003
917.804′2′0922—dc21
                              2003004343

Jacket image: *Lewis and Clark at Three Forks* by Edgar S. Paxton (detail).
Used by permission of the Montana Historical Society.
Design by Angela Schmitt

For My Grandchildren
Diane, Evan, and Nakoa

Contents

Illustrations

Acknowledgments

Many hours of research in the William Robertson Coe Library and American Heritage Center at the University of Wyoming went into the making of this book. I am grateful to the staff of the Coe Library, as well as the William E. Morgan Library at Colorado State University, and the Special Collections room at New Mexico State University, and thankful for their extensive collections of western history.

Thanks are due to the Auburn-Placer County Library of Auburn, California, for a copy of Jean Baptiste Charbonneau's obituary in *The Placer Herald;* to Kerry Samson of that library for information about the Orleans Hotel; to Kathy Hodges of the Idaho State Historical Society for a copy of Baptiste's obituary in *The Owyhee Avalanche;* and to Ila Harner, city clerk and treasurer of Jordan Valley, Oregon, for help in finding the burial site of Baptiste.

Orlan Svingen of the Washington State University History Department and Roderick Ariwite of the Lemhi Shoshone tribe were helpful regarding the Lemhi Shoshone people. Viola and Kelly Anglin of the Tendoy Store in Tendoy, Idaho, guided us around Sacagawea's birthplace.

At the Lewis and Clark Trail Heritage Foundation, Donna Phillips of the Genealogical Committee discovered information on the question of Toussaint Charbonneau's birth date. Librarian Julianne Ruby and Martin L. Erickson, then editor of *We Proceeded On*, the foundation's magazine, provided copies of articles.

My notes and bibliography will show how much I owe to men and women more learned than I who have plowed this ground before me. The conclusions I reached are, of course, my own.

My wife, Joyce Miller Nelson, helped me to see the Charbonneaus, not only as key figures in great events of American history, but as living human beings.

Introduction

In the half year since he became superintendent of Indian affairs for Louisiana Territory, Joshua Pilcher had felt himself pestered by visitors to his cluttered office off Pine Street in St. Louis.

But when he spotted the stooped, shaggy man who wandered up the stone walk on October 21, 1839, Pilcher welcomed a companion from his well-remembered days as a fur trader.

The caller was Toussaint Charbonneau, interpreter to Captains Meriwether Lewis and William Clark, husband to Sacagawea, and father to Jean Baptiste. Together and separately, the three were actors in events that would leave an indelible mark on the American West of their time.

To Pilcher, however, Toussaint was simply an old acquaintance he was glad to see again.

The Indian affairs superintendent, a one-time St. Louis banker, was president of the Missouri Fur Company when he met Charbonneau. Later he became an Indian agent under William Clark, then the superintendent at St. Louis. He soon began to think that the aging frontiersman was no longer up to the job and, when Clark died on September 1, 1838, he jumped at the chance for promotion.

Once he was installed in the superintendent's two-room office, he had second thoughts.

Pilcher's waspish, mercurial temper was frayed by long hours at his desk, the problems of hiring good help on a limited budget, and the flood of paper work.

But most of all the visitors.

Destitute Indians arrived seeking help. Entrepreneurs came by trying to sell him land for distribution to the tribes. Friends dropped in to chat.

When would they give him any peace?

He paid attention, though, to Charbonneau.[1]

The old frontiersman was not just passing through, nor had he dropped by from any office in St. Louis. He had traveled 1,600 miles from the villages of the Mandan and Hidatsa Indians on the upper Missouri River.

He had a grievance. For twenty years he had been a government interpreter with the Mandans and Hidatsas, appointed by William Clark. Clark had befriended Charbonneau and his Indian wife Sacagawea when they were together on the great expedition of 1804 to 1806—Clark as co-captain, Charbonneau and Sacagawea as interpreters.

The need for an interpreter at the villages was now questionable at best. A smallpox epidemic had all but wiped out the Mandans. The fur trade with the Indians was dwindling. Nevertheless, Clark kept his old friend on the job.

With Clark's death, the government decided Charbonneau was no longer needed. As of the end of 1838, he was off the payroll.

But nobody bothered to tell Charbonneau. At his remote outpost on the Knife River near present-day Bismarck, North Dakota, the news of his dismissal did not reach him until July, 1839.

Amid the jumble of ledgers, boxes, and fireplace tongs in his office, Pilcher listened to the words of an old man who wanted his six months' pay. Five days later, he wrote to Indian Commissioner Carey A. Harris in Washington.

Charbonneau, he said, "came into the office, tottering under the infirmities of eighty winters, without a dollar to support him, to ask what appeared to me to be nothing more than just."

The interpreter had been, noted Pilcher, "a faithful servant of the Government —though in a humble capacity." He "rendered much service" as a member of Lewis and Clark's Corps of Discovery. He provided intelligence about British efforts to gain Indian allies during the War of 1812. He served on expedition after expedition as American influence spread farther and farther west.

"I accordingly have paid his salary . . . for the 1st and 2nd quarters of this year," the weary bureaucrat wrote, "with the understanding that his services are no longer required."

By 1843, the man who was no longer required would be dead. Somewhere along the line, he had acquired some property, because his son, Jean Baptiste, by then himself a veteran of expeditions into the West, sold it that year for $320.

The scene in Pilcher's office was the last for Toussaint Charbonneau on the stage of history, one that he had entered three and a half decades before on a cold autumn day in his adopted homeland.[2]

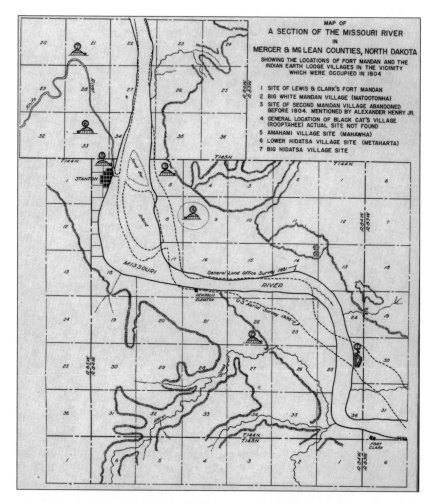

Map of the section of the Missouri River where the Lewis and Clark party spent the winter of 1804-1805. No. 6 near the top of the map is the village where Sacagawea and Toussaint Charbonneau lived. No. 1, near the southeast corner, is Fort Clatsop, where Jean Baptiste Charbonneau was born. Fort Clark, where Toussaint endured harsh conditions in later life, is shown below it. (Courtesy of the State Historical Society of North Dakota NDH Quarterly vol. XIV January-October 1947.)

The Meeting

The sound of axes and saws was in the air when the talkative French-speaking stranger rode into the well-wooded site on the east bank of the Missouri River. William Clark had chosen the site as a winter camp for President Thomas Jefferson's expedition to find "the most direct & practicable water communication across this continent."[1]

Sunday, November 4, 1804, was a fine, clear day, but there was no Sabbath break for Clark, Meriwether Lewis, or their forty-three men. Under the leadership of Sergeant Patrick Gass, a burly dark-hued Irishman who had been a carpenter in Pennsylvania before joining the Army, they had been at work all weekend cutting down cottonwood trees and building cabins, stuffing the cracks with rags, grass, and mortar.[2]

It had been a hard five-and-one-half months of paddling, poling, and pulling their boats up the river from a camp near St. Louis to the one they were building on the east bank of the river close to the Mandan Indian villages. They had made the trip in a keelboat, a flat-bottomed covered vessel used to carry freight on a river, and two pirogues, or canoes made from hollowed tree trunks, one of them red and one white. Now they needed to hurry. There had been frost on the ground that morning. At midweek, a fierce northwest wind had given them warning that the brutal winter of the Knife River country was on its way.[3]

But the explorers took time to talk with their visitor. His name was Toussaint Charbonneau, and he had something they needed. He could speak the language of the Hidatsa Indians, a tongue much different from that of other Native Americans. It was so difficult that Charbonneau would admit years later he never did learn to pronounce it very well.[4]

It is no wonder the explorers were on the lookout for interpreters. When Lewis wrote four months earlier to enlist his old army companion Clark in his western venture, he said that a study of the "languages, traditions and monuments" of the tribes would be an important part of their task. He had obviously discussed this with Jefferson, as the president used precisely the same words in his instructions to Lewis, dated the day after Lewis's letter to Clark. For years, Jefferson had been collecting vocabularies of Indian languages and dialects. Lewis knew no Indian languages. Jefferson was telling him that a good interpreter would be needed.[5]

Lewis's first choice for an interpreter was as different as he could be from Charbonneau. Before he had gone further west than Lancaster, Pennsylvania, Jefferson's hand-picked explorer accepted an offer from John Conner, a trader with the Shawnee and Delaware Indians at a post in present-day Indiana. Conner was twenty-eight, more than a dozen years younger than Charbonneau. He was literate, while Charbonneau signed his name with an "X." Perhaps most importantly, Conner had spent his life east of the Mississippi. Charbonneau knew at least some of the country the explorers would traverse. The deal with Conner didn't work out, and Clark, at least, thought that was just as well.

"I do not think the failure in getting him is very material," he wrote.[6]

The explorers had found Charbonneau at one of the great crossroads of the North American fur trade. Since the middle of the seventeenth century, Mandan and Hidatsa people had lived in large villages along the Missouri. The villages became important centers for intertribal swapping of furs, robes, foodstuffs, horses, and ornaments, and soon attracted white traders.[7]

Charbonneau lived with the Hidatsas, in their cluster of substantial earthen lodges along the mouth of the Knife, and had just returned from a hunting trip with them when he met Lewis and Clark. He said he wanted to hear about the captains' meeting a few days earlier with the chiefs of the five Mandan and Hidatsa villages. He also offered his services as an interpreter. Nothing was put in writing, but the offer was accepted. Charbonneau became a provisional member of the Corps of Volunteers of Northwest Discovery.[8]

The new interpreter was at least three years older than Clark, seven years older than Lewis and ten years older than most members of the Corps, and he had a pregnant wife. But the prospect of a journey into the unknown at his time of life did not faze him. Toussaint Charbonneau was eager to go. His pay would be twenty-five dollars a month, the same as that of George Drouillard, an experienced Missouri frontiersman who months earlier had been hired as an interpreter and hunter. The monthly pay of interpreters was three to five times that of the other members of the Corps. They ate with the captains, just as interpreters dined at the table with the bourgeois, or head man, and his clerks at fur trading posts.[9]

In addition to his skill with the Hidatsa language, Charbonneau offered to bring one of his two Indian wives along on the expedition to serve as an interpreter with the Shoshone, or Snake, Indians whom they would meet later. They would be "interpreter and interpretress," said Clark. The name of the interpretress was Sacagawea. Private Joseph Whitehouse said she was "employed" as an interpreter, but records do not show that she was paid. Sacagawea was not present when Charbonneau met with the two captains. She made her appearance a week later, bringing buffalo robes for the officers. These arrangements brought together four diverse individuals whose names would forever be linked with the historic journey to the Pacific Ocean and back.[10]

Blue-eyed, fair-haired Meriwether Lewis was born on August 18, 1774, in the comfortable plantation society of the Virginia Piedmont. Before being named to head the expedition, he served as Thomas Jefferson's secretary. From boyhood, the moody, studious, bow-legged Meriwether had liked to take long solitary walks in the woods. Red-haired William Clark, already a veteran frontiersman, was also born in Virginia, on August 1, 1770, but moved to Kentucky as a small boy. He entered the army, and for a brief time Lewis served as an ensign in a rifle company under his command.[11]

Charbonneau was born about 1758 in or near the little religious and fur-trading center of Ville-Marie, later to become Montreal. The fur trade dominated the Canadian economy, and young Toussaint broke into it as a common laborer for the tycoons of the North West Company—delivering rum, tobacco, knives, and other trade goods to Indian camps from posts the company built along the Assiniboine River. During these years, a young German immigrant named John Jacob Astor was trudging through the same woods, often with a pack on his back, ferreting out secrets that would make him the kingpin of the Great Lakes Fur Trade. Like the better connected Astor, the energetic French Canadian Charbonneau wanted to improve himself. By 1796, he was in the Mandan villages, and was no longer anybody's lackey. He was a free trader, operating independently of both the North West Company and the rival Hudson's Bay Company.[12]

Charbonneau would boast in his old age of being "the only White man" in the villages when he arrived there to take up his new life among the Indians. Maybe his memory was faulty. Or perhaps he was exaggerating. He sometimes did stretch facts a bit. In the joking fireside manner of the traders, he told several people that when he arrived on the Missouri it was so small he could straddle it. At any rate, the half-Indian Rene Jusseaume, who would also become an interpreter for Lewis and Clark, led a North West Company expedition to the villages in the fall of 1794, well before Charbonneau's arrival. And long before Jusseaume's arrival, probably in about 1778, a man known to history only as Menard appeared. First white man or not, it was a new life for Charbonneau. He found Indian companions who plowed their fertile fields of corn and squash with the shoulder blades of the buffalo, and dug smoky brown flint from bowl-like depressions along the Knife River to tip their arrows for the hunt.[13]

Sacagawea's birth date was most likely 1788, a few years before Charbonneau settled at the villages. As a child of a Shoshone band to which later settlers would give the Mormon name Lemhi, she lived far away in the Rocky Mountains (probably near Tendoy, Idaho, close to a monument that now marks her birthplace). Each fall, the semi-nomadic Lemhi went eastward to the Three Forks of the Missouri to hunt buffalo. Often they were attacked by Hidatsas out to make war and steal horses. Sometimes, Lemhi children were along. Sacagawea was on one such trip in 1800, when she was about twelve. As a Hidatsa party came in sight, the hunters retreated and tried to hide in a wooded area about three miles up the north fork. The Hidatsas followed and attacked them, killing four women, four men, and several boys. Sacagawea waded into the river at a shallow point and headed for one of the islands that dot the stream in the area, but was captured in mid-flight. She and her companions were taken to the Hidatsa village to be slaves. Sacagawea caught the eye of Charbonneau, who made her one of his wives. Customs varied from tribe to tribe, but generally called for a ceremony, which often included instructions to the bride on wifely duties including fidelity.[14]

Sacagawea is one of the most familiar figures of the Lewis and Clark party. She has been perceived as an early-day heroine of the struggle for women's rights and remembered in countless paintings, statues, and stories. Lakes and mountains have been named for her, and she has been commemorated in a cantata, an intermezzo, and the sterling silver on a battleship. Recognition for Charbonneau has been less impressive. A clothing store in Bozeman, Montana, does bear his name, and a glossy residential development near Portland is named for his and Sacagawea's son, Jean Baptiste, who died in Oregon.[15]

A 1926 *Collier's* magazine article by the western journalist George Creel described how the Shoshone teenager "led Lewis and Clark up the wild reaches of the Missouri and over saw-toothed ranges; when the white captains wandered hopelessly amid enormities of granite, her unerring instinct found a way." Creel's elaborate fantasy was one of many. Similar accounts appeared in newspapers when a symbolic likeness of Sacagawea was chosen for a one dollar coin in 1998. It is a romantic and appealing picture, but the journals of the expedition do not support it. Sacagawea did provide valuable information on two occasions, when they were passing through country she remembered from childhood. For the most part, though, she probably knew less about most of the route than the two captains did. They had seen some maps, however imperfect, and collected all the information they could get from Indians and traders. Sacagawea proved a resourceful and hardy traveler as well as an interpreter, but except on rare occasions she was not a guide.[16]

Nor is it known what she looked like. She is said to have been lighter in complexion than Charbonneau's other wife, but there are no paintings or drawings done from life. As for Lewis and

Clark, their instructions from Jefferson were to make "observations . . . with great pains and accuracy" of what they saw along the route. He didn't tell them to describe members of their own party, and they didn't bother, so we know little about the appearance of any of them. Some travelers described the young Shoshones as among the best looking Indian women they saw, so it is likely Sacagawea was at least fairly attractive. Presumably she dressed in Mandan fashion, wearing a long garment of doeskin or mountain sheepskin with a fringed hem just below the knee. The dress was belted at the waist and form fitting above, except in the case of nursing mothers. Since Sacagawea was pregnant, her costume would soon be loosened above the girdle.[17]

Even the pronunciation and meaning of her name have been in question. The explorers, not great at spelling, wrote it out in their journals as Sahcagahweah or variations of that form. Nicholas Biddle and Paul Allen, whose 1814 narrative of the expedition was based on the journals, changed it to Sacajawea, the name which for years was adopted by most writers. The United States Geographic Board, in naming a mountain in Wyoming for her in 1933, said that Sacagawea is the correct spelling, as the Hidatsa language does not contain a "j" sound. The word is pronounced with a hard "g" and the accent on the broad "a" in the second syllable. It is generally believed to be a Hidatsa name meaning Bird Woman, "Sacaga" for "bird" and "wea" for "woman." Many Shoshone Indians, however, maintain it is a Shoshone word meaning "boat launcher" and spell and pronounce it as Sacajawea. The Hidatsas pronounce it with a hard "g." North Dakota has applied the spelling Sakakawea to a statue on the state Capitol grounds and the state's largest lake. In 2002, as the bicentennial of the expedition approached, the North Dakota State Library switched to Sacagawea, but other state organizations did not.[18]

Lewis himself set the tone for much of the later commentary about Charbonneau, describing him as "a man of no peculiar merit" who "was useful as an interpreter only, in which capacity he discharged his duties with good faith." Elliott Coues, one of the early editors of the explorers' journals, went further, calling him "a poor specimen . . . a tongue to wag in a mouth to fill," "the wretched Charbonneau," and one member of the party "who could have been lost without inconvenience." Coues did acknowledge that Toussaint "seems to have been good-natured, and meant well no doubt." He pictured Sacagawea as "wonderful," "the best of mothers," and a "remarkable little woman" who "contributed a full man's share to the success of the Expedition, besides taking care of her baby." Even had he been a saint, thought Coues, Charbonneau would have been by no means the equal of his wife. Prejudice may have played a part. One later writer commented, "As far as Coues is concerned, this Frenchman, because he is French, is a laggard and a coward." In a 1950s Hollywood version of the expedition, *The Far Horizon*, Charbonneau is cast as the villain. But there is more to be said. Not long before he joined Lewis and Clark, Charbonneau held a responsible position at Fort Pembina, a fur trading post in the extreme northeastern corner of present North Dakota.[19]

Clark, a shrewd judge of men, spoke well of his service on the expedition, as did later travelers who employed his services. David Meriwether, a future territorial governor of New Mexico for whom Charbonneau worked as an interpreter on the western plains, said, "though he was an old man when I first saw him, I derived much assistance from his council when I first embarked in the fur trade."[20]

He seems to have been a poor and timid sailor and hiker, not good qualities for a man on a transcontinental trek, but a good enough interpreter, and frequently a valuable source of the kind of information about the Indian tribes that Jefferson wanted his explorers to gather. He was also a good cook, certainly a skill to be prized by a group of men traveling across a wilderness.

As a free trader, Charbonneau obtained goods from North West and Hudson's Bay posts on credit, traded them with the Indians, and repaid the companies with the furs he obtained. Such men came to be called "residenters." They lived with the Indians, adopted their way of life, and curried favor by giving presents to the chiefs. Trading with the Indians was hard work. The traders had to carry a wide variety of goods, as tribes had different tastes in blankets, beads, knives, and other trade goods. Some traders carried liquor, but rationed it carefully to keep the Indians from getting drunk and causing trouble.[21]

In his long life, Charbonneau took many Indian wives, in ceremonies recognized as valid both by the Indians and the whites, but not necessarily as lifetime contracts. Asked in his later years about love life among the tribes, he was reported to have said that "the Indians generally are not as fond of women as we are," and added, "The women . . . with whom we had anything to do were not deficient in ardor."[22]

In December, 1794, John McDonnell, the North West Company clerk at Fort Esperance on the Qu'Appelle River, a branch of the Assiniboine, said Charbonneau and two other men were courting a notably beautiful young Indian woman. Charbonneau apparently did not succeed in this courtship. Two months later he was beaten with a canoe-carving tool by a woman who said she caught him raping her daughter. He was hardly able to walk back to his canoe. The prudish McDonnell, nicknamed "the Priest" by some in his company, said Charbonneau's beating was "a fate he highly deserved for his brutality," but nobody knows what really happened. McDonnell was contemptuous of all free traders, lapsing into French and calling them "Canaille," or riffraff.[23]

Certainly Charbonneau did not treat women with the courtliness customary in the Virginia Piedmont. In a wilderness camp at Rattlesnake Cliffs on the Missouri headwaters, Clark would rebuke him for striking Sacagawea at dinner. But that one sentence

—"I checked our interpreter for striking his woman at their Dinner"—hardly supports some writers' descriptions of him as an habitual wife beater. At worst, he seems to have been no worse than many men of his time and place.[26] Charbonneau made friends among the Indians, who thought up five names for him. Variously, he was Chief of the Little Village, Man of Many Gourds, Great Horse from Abroad, and Forest Bear. A fastidious observer described the fifth name simply as "not very refined."[24]

An estimated 3,600 Mandans and Hidatsas, more than the population of St. Louis at the time, lived in three villages along the Knife River. One visitor likened their earthen huts to "a cluster of molehills." Another found them so closely spaced that it was hard to pass between them. Still, they were impressive structures. Their domed roofs were supported by four cottonwood pillars with cross

The Interior of the Hut of a Mandan Chief by Karl Bodmer. Toussaint Charbonneau and Sacagawea lived in one of these impressive structures, which one visitor likened to "a cluster of molehills." Theirs was perhaps less imposing than the chief's. (Rare books Division, The New York Public Library, Astor, Lenox, and Tilden Foundation)

beams. Beds consisted of a sort of square case made of skins and blankets, located against the circular outer wall. The human inhabitants and their horses and dogs shared a dirt floor carpeted with buffalo robes. There was a hole at the top to let out the smoke, or at least most of it, from the fire built in the lodge's center. Charbonneau and Sacagawea lived in one of these lodges, in Metaharta, the middle village of the three both in size and in distance from the mouth of the Knife. Although it was not the smallest—it had about eighty warriors—it was called "the little village."[25]

On the evening of November 20, the husband-and-wife team of interpreters moved into Lewis and Clark's fortress-like camp downstream and across the Missouri. Charbonneau was preparing for an epic journey, but he would call "the little village" home for most of his life.[26]

CHAPTER TWO

Winter

Little more than three weeks after Toussaint Charbonneau met Lewis and Clark, the explorers were haggling over his services with an agent of the North West Company.

Traders from the fur-trading company and the Hudson's Bay Company were following their usual schedule. Pelts were in prime condition from fall into early spring, and that was when the traders came to bargain with the Indians.[1]

On November 24, Francoise-Antoine Laroque stopped by at Toussaint's Hidatsa village. Although Laroque was only twenty years old, this was not the first time he had made the long trip to the Knife River from Quebec. He had hired Charbonneau as an interpreter before, and wanted to again. But a Hudson's Bay trader was already on hand in the village, and told him the interpreter had moved to Fort Mandan to work for Lewis and Clark.

The next morning, Laroque saddled up and headed for the Americans' fort. As it turned out, he met Lewis on the way. Laroque had been educated partly in the United States and had adopted English as his preferred language, so their quarter-hour conversation went easily. Lewis invited Laroque to his cabin and, the trader thought, seemed friendly.

Already, though, there were signs of strain. The Hidatsas had heard rumors that the Americans were going to attack them, and their suspicions deepened when Toussaint moved into Fort Mandan. Clark thought they might have deepened further when Laroque's interpreter, Baptiste LaFrance, "took it upon himself to speak unfavorably of our intentions." Lewis told the Indians there was no truth to the rumors, and Clark made it clear to Laroque that he wanted no more such talk.[2]

Laroque still needed someone to interpret for him, particularly as the Hudson's Bay traders already had an interpreter who spoke the Hidatsas' language. He asked Toussaint to join him. Toussaint said he could not do so without Lewis's permission, and Laroque should speak to Lewis. Lewis and Clark had their own work for their interpreter to do, but said it was all right for him to help Laroque at times when they did not need his services. Because they were still suspicious of Laroque's attitude toward Americans, they cautioned Toussaint sternly not to say anything unfavorable about the United States or its citizens, even if Laroque ordered him to. Toussaint agreed.[3]

Laroque thought this settled the matter, and returned to the Mandan village to await his interpreter. Two days later Toussaint still had not arrived. It was snowing hard and blowing by now, and Laroque thought that was probably the reason for the delay. But when the weather cleared on the evening of November 29 and Toussaint still did not come, he set off to find out what the trouble was.[4]

Laroque arrived at Fort Mandan just as Lewis and Clark were dispatching a man to fetch him. They had heard disturbing news that the North West Company agent planned to give flags and medals to the Indians. They impressed upon Laroque that he was

Reconstructed Fort Mandan, Lewis and Clark's camp for the winter of 1804-1805. Sergeant Patrick Gass, a carpenter by background, supervised its construction of cottonwood trees stuffed with rags, grass and mortar. (Courtesy of the National Park Service, Lewis & Clark Interpretive Center, Great Falls, Montana)

in American territory, and no foreign flags or medals were to be given. Laroque told them he had no flags or medals and so "Ran no Risk of disobeying those orders." Clark seemed unconvinced. He noted in his journal only that Laroque "gave fair promises."[5]

The next day, Laroque returned to the Indian village. But just as Toussaint was setting off to join him, the interpreter's orders were changed. A band of Sioux had killed a Mandan the day before. Clark was taking twenty-three men to help the Mandans repulse their enemies, and Toussaint was ordered to accompany him. When they reached the Mandans' village, the Indians told them the Sioux had already gone home. They said they would be glad to join the Americans in pursuit of them in the spring, after the snow had melted. Clark, feeling that his show of force had merely made him ridiculous in the Mandans' eyes, counseled a more peaceful course and went back across the river to the explorers' camp.[6]

"Capt. Clark's expedition did not succeed, and Charbonneau joined me here this morning," a satisfied Laroque noted in his journal the next day. One of Toussaint's first tasks was to translate for Laroque when he met with Chief White Wolf in his lodge and, as the trader put it, "Harangued him etc." The words were probably not as hostile as this made them sound; "Harangue" was a term in common use on the frontier for any kind of speech-making.[7]

There were many such trading forays, especially as Laroque continued leery of being outdone by his rivals. On the evening of December 5, Toussaint and another of Laroque's men were ordered to follow a Hudson's Bay trader and an Indian as they headed into the woods in snowy, blustery weather with bundles on their backs. It turned out to be a false alarm. Toussaint and his companion soon met the Hudson's Bay pair, who had turned back because they did not find any Indians.[8]

On December 6, the six-day leave that Lewis and Clark had given Toussaint was up, and he returned to Fort Mandan. Laroque sent with him a note to the explorers thanking them and asking more of their interpreter's time whenever he could be spared.[9]

Like all free traders, Toussaint traded furs to both the North West Company and the Hudson's Bay Company, in return for credit with their outposts. On December 10, he brought Laroque the skins of seven wolves, one otter, and eighteen kit foxes. Laroque paid him by giving him a cotton shirt, a pair of corduroy trousers, and one other small article on credit. The exchange hardly seems a fair one, but Toussaint was already in debt to the company. Laroque needed an extra horse, as he was planning to return to Canada. So he persuaded Toussaint, who had two horses, to give him one of them as part payment of his debt.[10]

Meanwhile Toussaint may have gotten into a scrape over a woman. An Indian with two wives was threatening to kill one of them because he was jealous of one of the interpreters. Laroque, who stepped in to calm the Indian down, didn't say which interpreter was involved. Whichever one it was, the wife had taken refuge in the interpreter's house. The unpleasantness apparently was soon patched up. On December 21, the Indian brought both of his wives to Clark's tent and "Showed great anxiety to make up with the man with whom his jealousy Sprung."[11]

By Christmas Day, the Corps' triangular stockade was completed, and the holiday was greeted at around seven A.M. with the discharge of the swivel gun and a round of small arms fire. Each man had a glass of brandy or whiskey and the American flag was raised, then a second round of spirits was served. There was dancing all day until nine o'clock. No women were present except for Sacagawea, Toussaint's other wife, and the Indian wife of Rene Jesseaume, a fellow interpreter. They were wallflowers, not asked to dance but treated to "the amusement of looking on."[12]

The day after Christmas, Laroque again was in need of Toussaint's services. He had just heard that a band of Indians was hunting a two days' march away, and without an interpreter he would get few furs; a French-speaking Hudson's Bay clerk named George Budge would be there competing with him. All the Indians knew Budge, and he understood and spoke their language. Laroque tried to persuade Toussaint to travel with him and interpret, but Toussaint chose to welcome in the new year of 1805 at Fort Mandan. He would return to Laroque on January 2.[13]

Tension between the American explorers and the Canadian traders was deepening. Laroque's relations with Lewis and Clark continued polite, though edgy. Toussaint was caught in the middle. In mid-January of 1805, he and Budge returned from a ninety-mile fur-trading expedition to Hidatsa lodges in the hills of what is now western North Dakota, bringing unwelcome news. Toussaint said Budge had been denigrating Lewis and Clark, and word was going around that the North West Company planned to build a fort among the Hidatsas. He also said that an arrogant Hidatsa chief had spoken slightingly of the Americans, "Saying if we would give our great flag to him he would Come to See us."[14]

In addition to their news, the traders came back with faces so frostbitten that the skin peeled off. It was no wonder. About the same time, at least two members of an Indian hunting party froze to death. Clark thought the Indians were able to bear "more Cold than I thought it possible for man to indure."[15]

Despite the bitter weather, Toussaint accompanied Clark and seventeen others on a hunting trip down the frozen river early in February. The first day, they trudged upstream to an island, killed no game and had nothing to eat. The second day, the hunting was better, so they dined on venison in an abandoned Indian lodge. The fourth day was the best hunting yet; nine elk and eighteen deer. Every man in the party was either hunting or collecting the meat—as much of it as escaped foraging wolves, ravens, and magpies—and packing it to camp.

On the next day, February 8, Toussaint and two others loaded the best of the meat on three horses and started for Fort Mandan. It was a forty-four-mile trek over ice and through knee-deep snow, in air so keen it froze men's ears. Eight miles from the fort, the unshod horses gave out, unable to walk any further on the ice. Toussaint left them on shore, still loaded with meat. He and his companions arrived at the fort on February 10. Lewis sent two sleds for the meat. Clark and the others continued the hunt, and staggered into the fort on February 12.[16]

On January 20, one of Toussaint's wives—probably Sacagawea, who was about seventeen years old and eight-and-one-half months pregnant—had begun feeling sick. Clark ordered his African-American slave, York, to give her stewed fruit and tea.

For some reason, this upset the hot-tempered Jusseaume, who got into a quarrel with Toussaint about it.[17]

On February 11, the day after her husband's return, Sacagawea gave birth to a baby boy. He was named Jean Baptiste, after Toussaint's father. It was Sacagawea's first child, and her labor was difficult. Jusseaume told Lewis he had frequently used a small portion of the rattle of a rattlesnake to hasten birth. As he often did, Lewis had doubts about Jusseaume's story. Nevertheless, he had a rattle with him and handed two rings of it to Jusseaume, who broke it into small pieces and gave it to Sacagawea with a small drink of water. When the baby arrived less than ten minutes later, at approximately five o'clock in the evening, Lewis conceded that the remedy "may be worthy of future experiment." The baby, he said, was "a fine boy." Sergeant Gass, returning the next day from a hunting trip, was pleased to note that "one of our interpreter's wives had in our absence made an ADDITION to our number."[18]

By mid-March, Toussaint was in trouble. After resting up, he had returned to Metaharta, where he could tell friends about his new son. On March 7, he returned bearing gifts from North West Company agent, Charles Chaboillez. Specifically, he brought two arms' length of scarlet cloth and one of blue, a pair of corduroy coats, one vest, a length of red cloth decorated with bars, 200 musket balls, a supply of powder, three knives, and some tobacco. These might have been a present for the new parents, but Lewis and Clark evidently considered them a bribe. The two captains had come to suspect—they had "every reason to believe," said Clark—that their interpreter was in league with the men of the North West Company and Hudson's Bay Company to prevent American incursions into the fur trade. They took Toussaint to task about it on March 11. But their interpreter was important to them, so they "gave him the night to reflect and determine whether or not he intends to go with us under the regulations stated" as a working member of the expedition.[19]

Toussaint, after a snowy night's deliberation, said he would not agree to the terms. He would not stand guard, and would refuse to do work "let our Situation be what may." There was some merit to his argument. Interpreters did not generally do menial work; Drouillard did not. Toussaint also said he would not be subject to the captains' orders, and would be free to leave the party if he was "miffed" with any member of it. He also asked that he be allowed to bring his trade goods with him. The captains said his conditions were unacceptable, and dismissed him. Their agreement, after all, had been only a spoken one. Veteran upper Missouri trader Joseph Gravelines was hired in his place.

Toussaint left the fort in anger and pitched a lodge outside the walls. "Charbonneau was cooler than the weather at Fort Mandan, and it is a wonder he was not frozen out of the garrison," commented Coues. However, there might be reasons for Toussaint's action that were not stated. He and Sacagawea could have had second thoughts about a journey halfway across the continent with a new baby.[20]

Three days later, Toussaint changed his mind. As he spoke virtually no English at the time, he brought a French interpreter, through whom he implored Clark to "excuse his Simplicity" and take him back. As neither Clark nor Lewis gave him any encouragement, he packed up and began transporting his baggage across the river, so he could return to the Hidatsa village. Presumably, Sacagawea and the baby were with him. On March 17, with most of his possessions already across, he sent the Frenchman to Lewis and Clark to reiterate his pleas, and the captains relented. They called Toussaint in for a talk, and he agreed to perform the same duties as the others. He brought his goods back and pitched a tent outside Fort Mandan. The following day, he signed an "X" beside his name, and formally became a member of the Corps of Discovery, effective as of the group's departure from Fort Mandan.

Already, the Missouri was beginning to thaw. As soon as the river was free of floating chunks of ice, it would be time to get going. The men set to work building six additional canoes from cottonwood logs. The keelboat was loaded with journals, maps and botanical and biological specimens, including a live prairie dog and several live birds, to be taken to St. Louis for shipment to Jefferson. Returning soldiers and others who had not been picked for the permanent party would man the keelboat. Gravelines was among them.[21]

There was thunder, lightning and rain on April 1, when Clark first had the boats put in the water. Going on into country unknown to them were the two captains, three sergeants, twenty-three privates, Drouillard, Toussaint, Sacagawea and her baby, and the slave York. Clark wrote that Toussaint's other Shoshone wife, the younger of the two, would also be in the party. For some reason, plans were changed. Sacagawea would be the only woman on the expedition.[22]

At about four P.M. on Sunday, April 7, the keelboat departed for St. Louis. Moments afterward, Clark and his men steered the canoes upstream. Lewis, the lover of solitary walks, decided that with so little daylight left, and the weather clear and pleasant, he would hike to their evening campsite. There, he shared a tent of dressed buffalo skins, tied Indian-fashion around ten or twelve poles, with Clark, Drouillard, Toussaint, Sacagawea, and her infant, not yet two months old. They would tent together for most of the time in the coming months.[23]

Against the Current

The Missouri River was a stern antagonist. Its murky water hid fallen logs, which on the trip up from St. Louis had snagged the keelboat and stove a hole in one of the pirogues. Often the men could make no headway with oars against the mainstream current, and sought calmer water near the shore. There they mounted a catwalk and tried to push the craft along with poles fitted against their shoulders. When even this didn't work, they would break out a long rope and walk along the bank with it, engaging in a grim tug of war with the mighty stream. Sometimes they just jumped into the river and pushed. Canoes would upset or fill with water when faced with rapids or beaver dams.[1]

It was no wonder that Toussaint, more experienced as a woodsman than a boatman, was in trouble before the expedition had been on the river for a week.

There was a foretaste on the first full day. Bucking a strong northwest wind, one of the canoes filled with water. Half a bag of biscuit and two-thirds of a barrel of gunpowder were soaked.[2]

On Saturday, April 13, with Toussaint at the tiller, a sudden squall threatened an even more serious loss. The wind had been favorable all day, and the explorers had ordered both the fore-and-aft spritsail and the smaller square sail hoisted on the white pirogue. They made good time until the squall came up about two P.M., turning the craft on its side.

Toussaint panicked and threw the pirogue with its side to the wind. The spritsail whirled so violently on its diagonal pole that the boat nearly overturned. Had it done so, its priceless cargo of instruments, papers, medicine, and trade goods would have been swept away by the Missouri. Lewis stepped in and ordered Drouillard to take over. With Drouillard's steady hand at the helm the sails were quickly taken in and the vessel was sailing before the wind again. "We fortunately escaped," Lewis said. Fortunate indeed. They were more than 200 yards from shore, amid high waves, with Sacagawea, her infant, and three men who could not swim. Lewis ordered that the boat go on with only its less vulnerable square sail in the wind.[3]

The next day Sergeant John Ordway noted in his journal, no doubt with relief, that the wind was "gentle from the South." It carried them past the mouths of two creeks that Toussaint recognized. They flowed into the Missouri just below an island that could hardly be missed. It was two-and-one-half miles long counting its sandbar. Toussaint said he had once camped on the uppermost of the two streams for several weeks with a Hidatsa Indian hunting party. Ordway said the interpreter "had been to the head of it which is further up the Missourie than any white man has been." Not quite. Toussaint said two Frenchmen who were with him lost their way and straggled a few miles farther. Although one of the Frenchmen, Jean Baptiste Lepage, was now part of their permanent party, the explorers could not determine how far the stragglers had gone. They named the stream Charbonneau Creek. The honor was not to last, however. It is now called Bear Den Creek.[4]

A few mornings later, Clark, vexed by needing to referee a squabble over a beaver caught in two traps, walked up a hill to clear his head. The river, he could see, took a deep bend toward the south near what is now the Montana border. Deciding to investigate, he took Toussaint with him. As Toussaint could not swim, he may well have preferred walking to the perils of the river. Sacagawea came along with the child Baptiste in her arms. There were many such walks. Sacagawea would bring the captain the yellow fruit of the Missouri currant, or wild licorice, or the turnip-like root vegetable that Lewis called the "white apple." As early as April 9, Lewis had written, "When we halted for dinner the squaw busied herself in serching for the wild artichokes which the mice collect and deposit in large hoards. this operation . . . soon proved successful and she procured a good quantity of these roots."[5]

Toussaint was proving himself worth his pay as a cook, making a sausage from diced buffalo meat that Lewis esteemed "one of the greatest delicacies of the forest." The campfire chef would take about six feet of the lower intestine of a buffalo and squeeze most—not all, the fastidious Lewis observed—of the contents out. Next he would knead some of the bison's shoulder muscle and other meat together with a generous amount of kidney suet. The fatty sausage, liberally salted and peppered and sprinkled with a little flour, was stuffed into the gut, which the cook tied at one end. After squeezing more of the intestine's original contents out, he tied it at the other end, rinsed it in the muddy river, boiled it in a copper kettle and fried it in bear's oil until it was brown. Then, said Lewis, it was "ready to assuage the pangs of a keen appetite or such as travelers in the wilderness are seldom at a loss for." The dish was, in the words of a later traveler, John Charles Frémont, "the chef d'ouvre of a prairie cook."[6]

Since Toussaint's mishap of April 13, Drouillard had usually been steering the white pirogue. On May 14, however, Toussaint was sitting in for him—"unfortunately for us," said Lewis, who described Toussaint as "perhaps the most timid waterman in the world." A strain of timidity was understandable in a non-swimmer piloting a clumsy flat-bottomed craft up the Missouri. But again the skilled woodsman Toussaint proved that he was out of his element on the water.[7]

As before, a sudden squall struck the boat. Instead of putting the vessel before the wind as a more experienced hand would have done, Toussaint steered her directly into it. This knocked the brace of the square sail out of the hands of the man attending it. The billowing sail turned the pirogue on its side, and the boat began to fill with water. Only the resistance of the sail bouncing on the water kept it from foundering.

The two captains generally avoided being ashore at the same time, but both were now on the opposite shore from the cargo-laden dugout canoe. "In this pirogue were embarked our papers, instruments, books, medicine, a great part of our merchandise and in short almost every article indispensably necessary," Lewis wrote that night. The two commanders fired their guns to attract attention and started shouting orders to cut the halyards and haul the sail. In the wind, they could not be heard. Desperate, Lewis threw down his gun and shot pouch and started unbuttoning his coat to plunge into the river. Fortunately, second thoughts prevailed. The pirogue was 300 yards away. In the waves and current, he would never have made it. The pirogue lay on its side for a terrible thirty seconds before the sail was taken in. By then, the boat had filled to within an inch of the gunwales. All was confusion, with Toussaint "crying to his god for mercy" and the nearly blind, fiddle-playing Pierre Cruzatte, in the bow, shouting orders to him to seize the rudder.[8]

Sacagawea, sitting in the stern with her infant in a basket-like cradle made of cord the explorers had brought, busied herself catching articles as they floated out. Lewis said that Sacagawea showed "equal fortitude and resolution with any person on board." Finally, with the waves running high and threatening to swamp the boat completely, Cruzatte threatened to shoot the steersman immediately if he did not do his duty. This worked, and Toussaint went to work to right the boat. Cruzatte ordered the other two men on board, neither of whom could swim, to start bailing with a couple of handy kettles. He and the two others then rowed the boat, still scarcely above water, ashore. The commanders oversaw the completion of the bailing and the removal of the contents. Then they took another measure they thought required by the circumstances, issuing each man a quarter pint of whiskey and taking a drink of grog themselves.[9]

The next morning, the soggy articles were stretched out on the ground to dry. But it was a cloudy, rainy day and there was a heavy dew overnight. The sun shone on the morning of May 16, and the goods were dry in time for the party to pack up and set off in mid-afternoon. The damage was not as bad as they had feared. Some of the medicine was spoiled or nearly so. Some papers and nearly all of the books were wet but still usable. Garden seeds and a little gunpowder were lost, and a few pots and pans had fallen overboard and sunk. Sacagawea had done her work well. Six days later, passing through what is now eastern Montana, they named a river for her. It was later called Crooked River, as the memory of the expedition faded, but still later was renamed Sacagawea River.[10]

The non-swimmer Toussaint had survived his second trial by water. Next came the trial by fire. Late on the night of May 17, the two captains and their interpreter and his family were roused from sleep by the guard on duty. A large tree had caught fire and was leaning precariously over the leather tent they shared. In moments they were outside, Sacagawea no doubt hugging her crying infant for protection against the brutal wind that was fanning the flames. The men managed to get the tent moved, and none too soon. The top of the burning tree fell on the spot where it had stood. "Had we been a few minutes later we should have been crushed to attoms," Lewis wrote in his journal. Even so the flames spread through surrounding trees, and the wind blew burning coals onto the tent. The tent was tattered, but no one was hurt.[11]

Members of the Corps of Discovery were also encountering the grizzly bear. Toussaint, hunting with Lewis and others, met a grizzly on June 2 below the mouth of a river Lewis named the Marias. The bear came very near to catching Drouillard. Toussaint, a less experienced hunter, at first fired his gun in the air as he ran, then wisely took cover in some bushes. Drouillard made the kill by shooting the bear in the head—the only shot, thought Lewis, "that will conquer the ferocity of those tremendous animals."[12]

At the mouth of the Marias, Sacagawea became ill. On the evening of June 10 and 11, Clark bled her, a common medical practice at the time that he thought helped. Later doctors believed the treatment may have worsened her condition, causing her fingers and arms to twitch from loss of minerals. Lewis believed Sacagawea's illness was an obstruction of the menses caused by a cold. One modern medical authority has speculated that she had a gonorrhea infection that caused chronic pelvic inflammatory disease. In any case, she was badly off. Three days in a row, Ordway noted in his journal that the interpreter's wife was "very sick." On June 12, her condition worsened. The explorers' compassion for the young woman and her child was mingled with their fear of losing their interpreter in the coming crucial negotiations with the Shoshones. They needed Shoshone horses to get over the mountains that lay ahead. [13]

Clark was caring for Sacagawea because Lewis, the commander for whom Jefferson had arranged instructions from the Philadelphia physician Benjamin Rush, and whose mother had been a well-known Virginia herb doctor, had gone ahead to map out their route. [14]

On June 13, the party reached an abandoned Indian fort in what is now Chouteau County, Montana. It must have been a difficult journey. Sacagawea continued to be very sick. Private Joseph Whitehouse was sick and had a bad headache, two men suffered from swellings and toothache, and another was feverish. Sacagawea complained all one night. In the morning, Clark concluded her condition was "excessively bad . . . somewhat dangerous." The next day, she was low spirited, but Clark thought she revived when he treated her with a bark poultice. On June 16, she refused all medicine until Toussaint, finding her out of her senses, persuaded her to take some. It apparently did no good. Clark wrote in his journal that "if She dies it will be the fault of her husband as I am now convinced." This seems unfair, since Toussaint was trying to help. It is also uncharacteristic of Clark, usually the more generous of the captains in his judgments of their interpreter. Possibly, he just made a mistake, and meant to write that Sacagawea's death would "not be the fault of her husband."[15]

When Lewis rejoined the party on June 16 and took over Sacagawea's treatment, he found her "much reduced." Her pulse was barely perceptible, and the twitching of her arms and fingers alarmed him. He sent hunters to collect water from a nearby mineral spring, but the delirious woman refused to take it until persuaded by Toussaint, again playing an important role in his wife's treatment. After drinking, she reported feeling less pain. Lewis continued Clark's poultices, which seemed to him to make her pulse strong and more regular. He also gave her a small dose of laudanum, a tincture of opium widely used to kill pain and help the patient sleep. He decided he would remain at the camp to treat Sacagawea and prepare for the portage around the Great Falls of the Missouri. Lewis controlled his patient's diet, allowing her to eat moderately of salted and peppered broiled buffalo and a rich soup of the same meat. By the seventeenth, Lewis was confident she would soon be well.[16]

Before long, Sacagawea was sitting up most of the day, and Lewis thought her strong enough that he gave her sulfuric acid as a tonic. She was able to walk out from the camp and on June 19 she picked some of the prairie turnips she was fond of. After eating a number of them raw, she followed up with dried fish. When her fever returned and she complained of pain, Lewis rebuked Toussaint. He had been told what his wife should and should not eat. The next day, Sacagawea's fever and pain abated and she was walking about and fishing. To Lewis, she appeared to be "in a fair way to recovery."[17]

Early on the morning of June 22, the two captains and most members of the Corps of Discovery hoisted one of their canoes onto the axles of an undercarriage and piled a heavy load of baggage on top of it. They had selected a camp site in the White Bear Islands area three miles above the falls. Toussaint and Sacagawea, along with Ordway, fisherman Silas Goodrich and the slave York, were left behind to look after the rest of the supplies.[18]

The advance party was finding the going rough. Men put double soles on their moccasins for protection against prickly pears, the cactus whose spines pierced their moccasins and feet. Carrying heavy burdens as they were, their feet hurt terribly. Some fainted. All had to rest often, and many fell asleep at each stop.[19]

Clark decided that everybody must help—"cooks and all." Nevertheless, Toussaint remained at the lower camp, providing hearty meals for the portagers as they set out on their day's work. Sacagawea, now recovered, was with him.[20]

On the morning of June 29, however, a heavy rainfall changed things for both of them and plunged them into perhaps the greatest danger from the elements that they were ever in. Clark had planned to get the rest of the baggage to the upper camp that day, but he knew the men would never make it over the soggy plain with their heavy burdens by nightfall. Then he had another idea. On an earlier hike, he had taken notes, but a gust of wind had blown them away. He decided to return to the upper camp by following the south bank of the river on foot, so that he could make notes again. Leaving one man to guard the baggage at the lower campsite, he took Toussaint, Sacagawea, and York with him. As they approached the falls, York spotted a herd of buffalo and set out to hunt them. To the west, a black cloud arose. They were in for more rain. At first, they could find no shelter that they could reach before running into strong winds. Finally, Clark spotted a deep gully a short distance above the falls with shelving rocks on its upper side to protect them. In this refuge, they felt safe enough that they laid down their guns, compass and other equipment.[21]

At first, the rain was moderate. Then an almost cyclonic wind came up, stronger than any of them had expected. Still, the ravine protected them. A few minutes later, the shower turned into the most violent rain and hail storm Clark had ever seen. "The rain fell like one volley of water." Turning to look up the gulch, they saw a torrent freighted with mud and large rocks rushing down upon them. As the captain reached for his rifle and ammunition pouch, the water climbed to his waist, soaking his valuable watch. Sacagawea had only time to sweep up her naked infant in her arms; Baptiste's clothing and the cradle in which she usually carried him were swept away. With his rifle in his left hand, Clark used his right to help Toussaint up the steep side of the ravine, pausing only to boost the Indian woman and her child. Clark described Toussaint as "much Scared and nearly without motion." Still, he scrambled up the bank, took his wife's hand and pulled her up as Clark pushed. They barely made it, the water rising to fifteen feet as they inched their way up the bluff. Lewis characteristically gave Clark all the credit and Toussaint none. "But for Captain Clark, both himself and his woman and child must have perished," he said. But had either Clark or Toussaint faltered, the current would have swept all of them into the river only a quarter of a mile above the eighty-seven-foot waterfall.[22]

Captain Clark, Charbonneau, Sacajawea, and Papoose in the Cloudburst near the Great Falls by C. M. Russell. They survived "as much as any men could, and live through it." (Watercolor painting, location unknown. Published in Olin D. Wheeler, *The Trail of Lewis and Clark,* 1904)

York, who had not seen them enter the ravine was searching for them. They were reunited with Clark on the top of the bluff. Clark, fearing a relapse for Sacagawea, gave up plans to go to the upper camp. She and her wet, cold child could get dry clothing at the lower site. He gave all in the party a bit of whiskey from a canteen York was carrying, and the shivering woman "revived very much."[23]

The next day, Clark sent two men to search for lost articles. They found Clark's compass, the only large one they had, in a mound of mud and stones near the mouth of the ravine. The captain had lost "an elegant purse", his umbrella, and some powder and shot. Toussaint had lost his gun, shot pouch, and a tomahawk. Sacagawea had lost her baby's clothes and the cradle in which she carried him. But they had survived, recorded Whitehouse, "as much as any men could and live through it."[24]

There was more to live through. On July 1, the Corps of Discovery struggled through large hailstones with the rest of the goods. Because of the heat, they were going nearly naked, with nothing on their heads. The portage had taken almost a month. To make matters worse, the Indians told them they would soon be out of the buffalo country. Lewis regretted the loss of this source of food and in particular lamented that the sumptuous sausages "will be irretrievably lost and Sharbono out of imployment."[25]

Toussaint seemed to be improving as a waterman. When they were ready to leave for their next camp twenty miles upstream, Baptiste Lepage, one of the men who normally manned the canoes, was ill, and Lewis sent Toussaint to paddle in his place. Lewis took a six-mile shortcut by land, taking Sacagawea with him. They were approaching country that she knew. On July 22, she told Lewis that the three forks of the Missouri were near and that this was an area where her people camped. Lewis feared running into dangerous rapids or falls, but Sacagawea assured him that the river would continue its gentle rippling. Still they saw no sign of the Shoshones. Clark decided to take a search party ahead, and ordered Robert Frazer and brothers Reubin and Joseph Fields to accompany him. He granted Toussaint's plea to come along.[26]

They reached the forks on July 27, stopped for breakfast and marched on through steep, rocky terrain. Toussaint may have regretted his decision to come. It was tough traveling. Clark's own feet became blistered and bleeding from prickly pear thorns. After two days, Toussaint twisted an ankle and could go no further. Clark left Toussaint and Joseph Fields, whose feet were also sore, at their night's camp. He, Reubin Fields and Frazer hiked twelve miles to a peak overlooking the present-day Boulder River. Although they were anxious to find Shoshones, they saw no signs that Indians had been around recently. Back at the forks, the handicapped Toussaint was nearly swept away by the brisk current. Only Clark's stout arms rescued him from at least a good soaking.[27]

On August 6, accompanied by Lewis and Toussaint, Sacagawea went on a four and one-half mile walk through the land she remembered so well, spotting such landmarks as a large limestone outcropping that the Shoshones called the Beaverhead. She pointed out the island where she had been captured, although, wrote Lewis, "I cannot discover that she shews any immotion of sorrow in recollecting this event, or of joy in being again restored to her native country." The phlegmatic captain, never as fond of Sacagawea as his co-commander, reflected that "if she has enough to eat and a few trinkets to wear I believe she would be perfectly content anywhere." After Clark came up with the boats, Lewis continued his walk, but Toussaint, still troubled by his ankle, climbed aboard, Sacagawea with him.[28]

Beaverhead Rock, a large limestone outcropping near the Three Forks of the Missouri that Sacagawea recognized from her childhood. (Courtesy of the National Park Service, Lewis & Clark Interpretive Center, Great Falls, Montana)

The hardy walker Lewis outdistanced the canoes. As he waited, alone and impatient, for Clark's arrival, he spotted Toussaint gamely struggling up the shore on foot. The canoes had made slow going on the twisting, rapid river, and Toussaint had abandoned them. Lewis decided to go off on foot again the next day to seek the elusive Shoshones. Toussaint was still anxious to go, and believed his ankle was recovered enough to stand the march. Lewis had his doubts, but agreed to take him.[29]

Toussaint continued to complain of his leg and was, said Lewis, "the cause of considerable detention to us." On August 5, the interpreter said he would be unable to walk very far. From their camp, they could see a timbered ridge about seven miles away over easy terrain. Lewis loaded Toussaint and the injured Gass up with meat, and directed them to wait on the ridge, so they could all have dinner together. When Lewis and Drouillard made their way to the appointed rendezvous, however, Gass and Charbonneau were not there. They shouted for them, got no answer, and after a two-mile hike through brushy country strewn with prickly pear, found them camping three miles downstream, dining on the meat they had been given. The little meat that was left over, noted Lewis, was "the first we had taisted today."[30]

By this time, Lewis had chosen the fork that came in from the southwest, which they called the Jefferson, as their route, concluding it would have the most water year-around. He headed up it, with Toussaint at his side, leaving a note for the others to join. As they walked, however, he and Toussaint heard Clark and his men talking and shouting. Approaching the source of the noise, they found that Clark had chosen the wrong river. He thought the Gallatin, the stream flowing rapidly from the southeast that was named for Jefferson's secretary of the treasury, would be the easiest fork to ascend. He had not found Lewis's note.[31]

Still desperately seeking the Shoshones, Lewis set out afoot right after breakfast on August 9 with three men. As his interpreter, he took Drouillard, who was adept at Plains Indian sign language. For Toussaint to be useful as an interpreter, they would have had to take Sacagawea with them. Two days into their trip, they spotted an Indian on horseback about two miles away, riding down toward them. Lewis advanced toward the Indian unarmed, crying out "tab-ba-bone," which Sacagawea or Toussaint had told him meant "white man" in Shoshone. The Indian turned, whipped his horse and disappeared into the brush. Apparently Lewis's information was wrong. The word may have meant "stranger."[32]

Hiking up Lemhi Pass in search of the elusive Shoshones, Lewis "did not despair of shortly finding a passage over the mountains and of tasting the waters of the great Columbia this evening." When he and his party reached the Continental Divide, however, he saw "immense ranges of high mountains still to the West of us." The rugged Bitterroots lay ahead. On the downward slope of the pass, however, the explorers finally made contact with the people they were looking for. Two Shoshone women, huddled in a steep ravine, led them to their tribe's nearby camp.[33]

The Lemhi were a small band, about 400 in number. Although they had no previous direct contact with white men, they had acquired horses from the Comanches of the Southwest, who obtained them from the Spanish in Mexico. They needed the horses for hunting and for war. They decorated them and equipped them with shields to protect them from arrows. Their horses were prized possessions.[34]

Seated on green boughs and antelope skin in a leather lodge, the explorers soon found that it would be no easy task to part the Indians from their horses. Their plight was real; they were subject to frequent raids by their much more numerous enemies.[35]

Clark, Charbonneau, and Sacagawea were still struggling up the Jefferson. On August 15, Toussaint and Sacagawea narrowly escaped rattlesnake bites as they trudged along the river bank.

Clark, who also had two near encounters with the reptiles, aptly named the area Rattlesnake Mountain.[36]

Two days later, a party of Indians rode down and told them that Lewis was waiting for them. They spent that night at a spot they called Camp Fortunate, near present Dillon, Montana. The Indians offered them two of their pack horses for the trip to the rendezvous. They had walked less than a mile when several Indians approached on horseback, accompanied by Drouillard, dressed in Indian garb. Sacagawea started dancing for joy and signed to Clark that these were members of her tribe.[37]

More surprises were to come. Sacagawea had scarcely stepped ashore from their canoe when an Indian woman appeared whom she recognized as the young girl who had been taken captive. Unlike Sacagawea, the girl had escaped her captors. Their embraces moved even the laconic Lewis. Their reunion, he said, was "really affecting."[38]

Once together again, the two commanders lost little time getting down to business in a circular shelter of willow bushes they built for the crucial negotiations with the Shoshones. The parley was delayed briefly, however. Sacagawea, who had taken her seat to begin interpreting, suddenly sprang to her feet. She had recognized Chief Cameahwait, seated on a white robe a few feet from her. She called him her brother, although he may have been a cousin. Throwing her arms and blanket around him, she broke into tears.[39]

After a brief talk, Sacagawea resumed her seat and went to work. Not until the council was over did she learn that most of her family were dead. The man to whom she had been betrothed as a child was living with the Shoshone band. More than twice her age, he had two other wives. He claimed Sacagawea was his, but he did not want her because she had borne a child by Toussaint.[40]

The process of interpreting was complicated. Sacagawea spoke in Shoshone to her fellow tribesmen and passed their words on in

Hidatsa to Toussaint. He relayed them in French to Francois Labiche, who told Lewis and Clark what had been said. It was not all encouraging. The Indians told them they would encounter huge falls, impenetrable cliffs and neither ample game nor timber large enough to make canoes. The two commanders explained the purpose of their mission and said they would trade with the Indians later for the horses they needed.

The trek might be harder than expected, but it appeared they would have their pack horses.[41]

Monument to Sacagawea , with mountain peak in far left background on which her kinsman, the Lemhi Shoshone Chief Cameahwait, is buried. (Photo by Joyce Miller Nelson)

Over the Top

Toussaint and Sacagawea were assigned an important task as the party prepared for the trek through the mountains. Clark picked eleven men to go ahead with him to explore whether the route was as bad as the Indians said, and to make canoes if they found a navigable river. The two captains agreed that they would also take the interpreter and his wife, but only as far as the Shoshone camp. Their job was to see that the Indians quickly made good on their pledge to bring horses to the camp at the forks. Three days later, Toussaint, Sacagawea, Cameahwait, and about fifty Shoshone men and their women and children arrived with the horses.[1]

Meanwhile, bargaining with the Indians got off to a brisk start. Lewis traded a uniform coat, a pair of leggings, some handkerchiefs, three knives, and a few other articles—worth about twenty dollars in U.S. money—for three horses. It was a good bargain. Both sides got things they needed. Clark and his party left the next morning, taking two of the horses. Lewis kept one.[2]

When Clark returned from the Salmon River, he reported he had found a place where they should be able to launch boats. It was eighteen miles away by a good road, but the river would be difficult. It would be better to go overland to a navigable stretch of the Columbia or to the ocean.[3]

Lewis was busy collecting the kind of ethnographic information that Jefferson and his learned friends were looking for. Through Toussaint and Sacagawea, he asked questions about the culture of the Shoshones. He wondered whether the title of chief was hereditary, as with European royalty. It was not; all Shoshone men were chiefs, and the one who enjoyed "the greatest share of confidence" was the principal chief. Many Shoshone men had more than one wife. A man's wives and daughters were his property and he was free "to barter or dispose of either as he thinks proper."[4]

The Shoshone people seldom punished their children, especially the boys, because "it cows and breaks the Sperit of the boy to whip him, and that he never recovers his independence of mind after he is grown." Lewis asked whether the Shoshones had venereal diseases, one of the questions Benjamin Rush had specifically wanted answered. "The information was that they sometimes had it but I could not learn their remedy; they most usually die with its effects," he said. They were great fishermen, chiefly for salmon, and were called "Salmon Eaters." Toussaint and Sacagawea were proving their worth as gatherers of Shoshone lore.[5]

On August 24, Lewis gave Toussaint "some articles," which the interpreter traded for a horse for Sacagawea. The next day, Lewis received troubling news. As they approached a narrow mountain pass and stopped for their noon meal, Toussaint casually mentioned to him that Cameahwait, the head chief, was planning to lead a party down the Missouri in search of game. Lewis was aghast. The Shoshones had promised to help haul the expedition's goods across the mountains to the Columbia River watershed and to trade them for supply horses. Toussaint's news threatened to leave them stranded where they were. Not only that, but the interpreter had kept the information to himself for several hours. Sacagawea had learned of the proposed hunting trip, presumably from her kinsman, in the morning and had promptly told her husband. Toussaint had not told Lewis until lunch time. The captain could not, he said, "forbear speaking to him with some degree of asperity." To Lewis, Toussaint was failing his obligation to the Corps of Discovery. Toussaint might well have seen himself as being helpful to his wife's people.[6]

Lewis set to work to repair the damage. He smoked a pipe with Cameahwait and two other chiefs , and "asked them if they were men of their words." The other chiefs said the hunting trip was all Cameahwait's idea, and they were against it. Cameahwait said he knew it was wrong, but game was scarce that summer and his people were hungry. His principal responsibility was caring for his people. But he said he would keep his word, and agreed to send a young man to the village to countermand his orders.[7]

Trading got under way seriously when the explorers reached a Shoshone village on the Lemhi River near present-day Tendoy, Idaho. Lewis quickly obtained twenty-two horses, and then the bargaining became harder. Clark obtained one horse by giving up a pistol, powder and balls for the weapon, and a knife. Toussaint seemed to do better, securing a horse for one red cloak. The soldiers under Lewis and Clark's command were dressed in blue uniform coats faced with red, but an interpreter would probably not have authority to trade one of these away. More likely, the coat was Toussaint's own. On at least two later occasions, he was seen wearing a red jacket. The interpreter's bargain brought their inventory to forty horses, which Clark observed would serve not only for transport but to "Eate if necessary."[8]

It might be necessary. The hunters were finding little game. In an eleven-mile march, they bagged only a couple of pheasants.

By September 2, the men were struggling over steep hillsides covered with loose rock. One horse fell and was crippled. Seven died. The men carried loads uphill for horses unable to make the arduous climb. They fought their way through thick brush. Their fingers ached. "The road bad," Private Whitehouse wrote in his journal. On September 4, after a night of heavy snow, the men woke to find their moccasins frozen hard.[9]

That evening, cutting north into what is now Ravalli County, Montana, they met Salish Indians. Nobody in the explorers' party spoke Salish. There was, however, a Shoshone boy who had been taken captive by the tribe and could speak the language with Sacagawea. He was added to the complex translation chain, and Sacagawea passed on through him the explorers' assurances that they came in peace. The Indians agreed to the captains' pleas that they swap healthy horses for some of the travelers' worn-out ones. The party now had forty good pack horses, plus three colts.[10]

On the clear, cold morning of September 6, the company began packing up for some of the most difficult days of their cross-continent journey. Their course was west over the Lolo Trail across the Bitterroot Range. It would take them three weeks to conquer what Gass called "the most terrible mountains I ever beheld." Clark's misgivings about the need for horse meat proved justified. Short of rations, the expedition members dined on one of their pack animals, calling a nearby stream Killed Colt Creek.[11]

On September 22 the explorers, exhausted and enfeebled by hunger, made their way down a precipitous ridge onto the bunch grass of the Weippe Prairie in present Clearwater County, Idaho. They camped that night at a Nez Perce Indian village on Jim Ford Creek, a tributary of the Clearwater River. Neither Toussaint, Sacagawea, nor any of the other interpreters could understand the Nez Perce language, so conversation between the Indians and their ragged, starved, bearded visitors was conducted in the sign language in which Drouillard was skilled. The Nez Perce gave them roots, berries, and salmon. After resting they set out afoot for a site Clark had selected on the Clearwater, five miles west of today's Orofino. There were two cottonwood trees there large enough to make canoes up to thirty-five feet long.[12]

On October 7, 1805, For the first time since they left Camp Dubois nearly seventeen months before, the men of the Lewis and Clark expedition enjoyed the comparative luxury of paddling downstream. It was not, however, easy going. On the first day they passed through ten rapids. Tempers were fraying. Three days out, Toussaint and the two Fields brothers got into an argument. Apparently somebody had taken offense at a joke. Most of the time, the men ate roots and dried fish, and complained of going without meat. Some cooked and ate dogs they had purchased from the Indians. Gass said it was only "some Frenchmen " who did this, without saying whether the camp cook—Toussaint—was among them. Clark said "all the Party . . . relished the flesh of the dogs," although he scorned such fare.[13]

On October 10, the party reached the confluence of the Clearwater River and the Snake, one step closer to the Columbia. Stopping at Indian villages to shop, they got along well with the Nez Perce. Clark believed his young friend Sacagawea helped convince the Nez Perce that their visitors' intentions were friendly. "A woman with a party of men is a token of peace," he concluded, as no woman ever accompanied war parties of Indians.[14]

Six days later, they reached the Columbia where the Snake empties into it near present-day Pasco, Washington. Whitehouse wrote that some of the Yakima and Wanapum Indians had "beads, and small pieces of brass and copper hanging about them, which they made signs to us, that they got them from White people, who live on a River lying to the North of this place, and that they also got some of them at the Mouth of this River." They also knew some English swear words. [15]

Reaching a stretch of rapids near present McNary Dam, Clark took Toussaint and Sacagawea with him on a walk downstream to get a look at the treacherous water before attempting to run it. The rapids were as bad as he had expected, but the canoes made it through.[16]

As they passed the Indian villages strung along the lower Columbia, Toussaint could make little use of his interpreting skill. Neither he nor Sacagawea knew the languages of the coastal tribes.

These Indians were very different from the ones Toussaint knew, and perhaps they got on his nerves. On a windy day late in October, the captains had "Some words with Shabono our interpreter about his duty." But they were approaching their goal. The Columbia was widening and there was coastal fog.

It rained all one night and for the next two days, an augury of things to come. Four months later, they would be eager to leave "this great Pacific Octean which we been So long anxious to See."[17]

Fort Clatsop

T oussaint Charbonneau's first glimpse of the Pacific Ocean came toward evening on November 18, 1805. It may have been his first sighting of any ocean. Or perhaps, between his birth near Montreal and his arrival at the Mandan villages, he had made it down the St. Lawrence River and seen the Atlantic.

The view he saw of the Pacific was a stunning one. He also had his first look at a California condor that Reubin Fields shot on their first day out. Three days earlier, the Corps of Discovery had settled in for a ten-day stay on the east side of what is now called Baker Bay on the Washington shore of the Columbia. On November 17, Lewis led a party to Cape Disappointment, a promontory at the northern lip of the river's mouth, and then several miles up the coast. That night, Clark announced he was leaving at dawn to make the same trip. Anyone wanting to go with him should be ready bright and early. Toussaint was among the ten or eleven men who responded. The others, Clark said, were "well Contented with that part of the Ocean & its curiosities which could be seen from the vicinity of our Camp." After their trip across the continent one can perhaps hardly blame them, but they missed a spectacular jaunt.[1]

It did not begin auspiciously. Clark and his men ran into cloudy weather all day and a little rain at night. They went around Baker Bay, first hiking on a sandy beach and then making their way over hills covered with evergreens and thick undergrowth. Reaching Cape Disappointment, they climbed 150 feet to the top of a rocky hill, believed to be McKenzie Head in the present Fort Canby State Park. From this point, the hard trudging and climbing was all worth it. "The men," said Clark, "appear much Satisfied with their trip beholding with estonishment the high waves dashing against the rocks & this emence ocian."[2]

Cape Disappointment, at the northern edge of the mouth of the Columbia River, where Toussaint Charbonneau got his first glimpse of the Pacific Ocean. ". . . beholding with estonishment the high waves dashing against the rocks and this emence ocian." The next day, Toussaint and his companions hiked along the Long Beach Peninsula, seen from North Head on the cape. (Photo by Bill Wagner, courtesy Long Beach Peninsula Visitors Bureau)

They camped that night among the ponds and evergreen woods of the shoreline just north of McKenzie Head. In the morning they stumbled across rock outcroppings onto a sandy beach. About ten miles north of Cape Disappointment, they turned back, cut through the woods and camped on the east side of Wallacut River. Late in the afternoon of the 20th they returned to the main camp, bringing with them the condor—nine feet across the wings and three feet ten inches from bill to tail. Gass, who had stayed at the camp, described the bird as "a remarkably large buzzard."[3]

Equally remarkable to the explorers was a robe of sea-otter skins that one of the Indians had and the captains wanted. Gass called it "the finest fur I ever saw." Lewis and Clark offered two blankets, but the owner said he would not take five. He wanted some of the blue beads that the Indians prized for decorating moccasins and other gear. The only blue beads in camp were on a belt that Sacagawea wore around her waist. The commanders traded her belt for the robe. Later they gave her a blue cloth coat, presumably one of their uniform coats. No one indicated whether Sacagawea was consulted about the transaction.[4]

In the increasingly dreary weather, the explorers' thoughts were turning to the need for winter quarters. At an evening meeting on November 24, the commanders asked their men where they thought it would be best to look. The majority opted for locating on the south side of the river, provided they found good hunting. Both captains agreed with this. Sacagawea also agreed, but specified it should be a place with plenty of wapato, a root plant something like a potato. Although both Sacagawea and York expressed their opinions, Toussaint apparently did not express his. Fragmentary notes left by Clark show only blanks after his name.[5]

On November 29, Lewis and five men braved showers of rain and hail and set off downstream in a small canoe to look for a site. The captain returned on December 5, saying they had found a location with prospects for good hunting a short distance up a river that flowed into the Columbia. The river is now known as the Lewis and Clark. By December 10, they were clearing ground for a stockade, using axe handles made from the wood of local crabapple trees. They called the stockade Fort Clatsop after the nearby Indian tribe, and blazed a seven-mile trail to the ocean.[6]

Christmas, 1804, at Fort Mandan had been sledding weather, with a light snowfall on December 24 and then clearing skies. At Fort Clatsop, one year later, it was rainy and unpleasant. Of the 106 days they were to stay there, it would rain on all but twelve. The sun would shine on six. But at least the stockade was nearly enough finished that the men could abandon their tents and move into the huts inside the walls in time for the holiday, as they had the year before. As at Fort Mandan, the celebration began with the firing of a gun at daybreak. But this time there was no liquor to cheer the men's spirits. The last of it had been doled out after

Toussaint and Sacagawea's reconstructed quarters, next to the commanders', at Fort Clatsop. The interpreter and his family were lodged with Lewis and Clark throughout most of the journey. (Photo by Joyce Miller Nelson)

the storm that nearly swept Clark, Toussaint, and Sacagawea into the Missouri just above the Great Falls. There was elk meat for Toussaint to cook, but not yet any salt to season it. The captains gave tobacco to the men who used it, and silk handkerchiefs to the others. Sacagawea gave her friend Captain Clark two dozen otter tails, made into a kind of shoulder covering that Lewis, while among the Shoshones, had praised as "the most eligant piece of Indian dress I ever saw."[7]

As if a bird with a nine-foot wingspan were not enough, a delegation of Clatsops came to the fort the night of December 29 and announced that a whale had washed ashore on the coast. Clark put together a thirteen-man party to go to the beach in two canoes and try to bring back some meat. He did not at first include Toussaint. Sacagawea, however, had never seen the ocean, let alone a whale. "She had traveled a long way with us to See the great waters," said Clark, "and that now that monstrous fish was also to be Seen, She thought it verry hard that She Could not be permitted to See either." The next morning, the Charbonneau family joined the others for an early breakfast and then set off for the beach with them.[8]

They ran into stormy weather in the bay where the river, which they called the Netul, joined the Columbia. Clark beached the canoes and they marched through the woods under a clear sky, the first in two months. They camped by moonlight around driftwood fires at the forks of a creek.[9]

The next day, Sacagawea had her first view of the ocean that she had so longed to see. The party had just climbed what Clark called "the Steepest worst & highest mountain" he had ever ascended, which is saying something for a man who had just crossed the Rockies. It was Tillamook Head, which rises 1,136 feet above sea level. It must have been terrifying for a young woman carrying a baby on her back. But neither she nor her husband flinched. Grasping bushes, the exhausted hikers hauled themselves up with the sea immediately under them on the right. After making their way through a tangle of logs and underbrush, they camped for the night in a grove of spruce and white cedar.[10]

The following morning, they scrambled through brush and thick clumps of ferns to reach the summit of Tillamook Head. From the summit they inched their way to a spot where Toussaint and Sacagawea shared, in Clark's words, "the grandest and most pleasing prospects which my eyes ever surveyed." They were probably on a rocky promontory later named Bird Point. To the north they could see Cape Disappointment, to the south a distant view of Cape Lookout forty miles away, and everywhere waves breaking against the rocky coast.[11]

On a sandy shore near present-day Cannon Beach, Oregon, they found the creature they were looking for, stranded on a large rock. Most likely a blue whale, it was impressive enough in size, measuring 105 feet. The local Tillamook Indians, however, had scalded the flesh from it and were busy boiling the blubber. The stripped skeleton was probably not what Sacagawea was hoping to see, and try as he might Clark could not talk the Indians into parting with more than a few gallons of oil and a small stock of blubber. The men pried off some jaw and back bones. At least they could take some souvenirs back to Fort Clatsop.[12]

With Indians causing much more trouble than the explorers had experienced at Fort Mandan, Toussaint was given an additional duty. He was ordered to accompany three guards on a nightly sunset patrol to expel all Indians except the few that the commanding officers permitted to remain. Despite his relative ignorance of the Indians' languages, Toussaint could communicate with them better than the other men. Lewis's order of January 1, 1806, said that members of the local tribes were to be accorded friendly treatment. Nevertheless, he said, "it shall be the right of any individual, in a peaceable manner, to refuse admittance to, or put out of his room, any native who may become troublesome to him." If the Indian refused, the sergeant in charge of the guard could use any means he found necessary to remove the intruder from the fort. He was cautioned only that he was not to take the Indian's life.[13]

Indian women were readily available, with the complicity of their menfolk, for sex with the men of the Corps. Once, a Clatsop who had received medical attention from the captains brought his sister as payment. The woman seemed eager to cooperate in this arrangement, but the two commanders rejected the offer. The mortified woman then moved in with Toussaint and his family, whose room was next door to the captains'. A number of men came knocking on the door, but they were turned away and the woman soon left.[14]

Toussaint earned a footnote in the annals of ornithology at the end of January, when he picked up a dead bird near the fort and brought it to Lewis. The commander immediately recognized the bird as of the same species he had spotted the previous September 20, in rugged country on the west slope of the Rockies. It was a varied thrush, a robin-like bird with black and orange plumage that is common in the Pacific Northwest.[15]

By March, the commanders and their men were anxious to be off on their return journey, but were a canoe short. So why not steal one from the Clatsops, who, after all, Lewis said, had stolen elk meat from them? Clark says the suggestion was made by several in the party, including one of the interpreters. This seems to point to either Charbonneau or Drouillard. It is impossible to say for sure which of them it was. At any rate, four men went over to a prairie near the coast on March 18 and returned that evening with a canoe belonging to the Clatsops. Finding that the Clatsop chief Coboway was visiting the fort, they hid it from him. The theft, uncharacteristic of the two commanders, seems particularly callous because Lewis had spoken of Coboway as a decent man who was kind to them.[16]

By March 23, foul weather had delayed departure for five days. The weather that morning was so bad that the captains debated whether to risk starting or order another postponement. About noon, the rain stopped. The men loaded the canoes and at one P.M., under a clear sky, the long homeward journey began.[17]

Homeward Bound

Toussaint Charbonneau found a friend in William Clark.

By the time the Corps of Discovery reached Fort Clatsop, Clark had nicknames for the interpreter's wife and child. He called Sacagawea "Janey" and called Baptiste "Pomp" or "Pompey." He often walked with the three of them on shore. He survived near-disaster with them in the storm above the Great Falls. He looked on the Pacific with them.

It was a friendship that would endure until Clark's death thirty-two years later.[1]

Now Toussaint and Sacagawea would accompany Clark on the return home, as the two captains went separate ways. They had decided at Fort Clatsop that Clark would go back by way of the Yellowstone River, exploring what the Hidatsas had described as "a country not yet hunted, and abounding in animals of the fur kind." Lewis would return by the way of the Missouri after exploring the "noble" Marias River.

Before any of this could be undertaken, the explorers must cross the Bitterroot Mountains again. They had started out too early, and they badly needed horses. It was the same story as on the way west. The Indians needed their horses for war and hunting. They would part with them only if they could get beads, and the explorers had traded away all their beads.[2]

On April 16, Clark took a party including Toussaint and Sacagawea across to Indian villages on the north shore of the Columbia to try again. Clark dispatched Toussaint to the Che-luck-kit-ti-quar villages and Drouillard to the village of the Skillutes to invite the tribes to trade. Delegations came to his camp from both villages and "delayed the greater part of the day" but traded no horses. In the end, by trading off blankets and other items, Clark managed to get a few good pack animals. Toussaint, with a better sense of what the Indians needed, obtained a splendid mare for a weasel skin, elks' teeth and a belt. But they were still short of horses. The rocky portage around The Dalles was more of a struggle than it needed to be.[3]

On April 22, they camped at the mouth of the Deschutes River. As they got under way at seven A.M. Toussaint's mare threw off its pack, then bolted, apparently spooked by the saddle and robe that were still in place. The horse dashed from the top of a bluff to an Indian village, dumping the encumbrances on the way. Two men helped Toussaint recapture his horse, finding the saddle but not the robe. The Indians denied having seen it. Lewis, convinced that one of the villagers hid it in his lodge, responded with a rare burst of temper. He sent Sacagawea with a message to Clark to send him reinforcements. He had decided he would burn the Indians' mat lodges if they did not deliver the robe. The disaster that this could have led to was averted when Labiche found the garment behind a pile of baggage at an Indian lodge. The party marched on to a village of Tenino Indians, a tribe with which they might fare better.[4]

Here, Toussaint bought another horse, giving a shirt, a tomahawk, and other items for it. That night, he was admonished to keep both his horses securely tied. By morning, however, they were loose. The captains inquired and found that the animals had not been made secure. One horse was found nearby, but Toussaint and Labiche searched the plains in all directions without finding the other. The captains, impatient at the delay, ordered the remaining pack horses loaded and set off. Along the way, Toussaint made a deal with an Indian traveling with them. He gave his shirt and two leather outfits of Sacagawea's, and acquired another horse to replace the lost one.[5]

On April 27, along the stretch of the Columbia where McNary Dam would later be built, Toussaint again let one of his horses go astray. It was recaptured, but the party's departure was delayed until nine A.M., unusually late for the early-rising explorers.[6]

On April 28, Sacagawea at last found someone she could talk with in her native tongue. Near the confluence of the Walla Walla River with the Columbia, the explorers encountered a Shoshone woman who had been taken prisoner by Walla Walla Indians and could speak both their language and her own. Before this, the captains had relied on Drouillard's skill at sign language to communicate with the Walla Wallas. Now the Indians could speak to their captive, she to Sacagawea, Sacagawea to Toussaint, and Toussaint to a French speaker who knew enough English to pass on the message to Lewis and Clark. Clark said they "Conversed with them for Several hours and fully Satisfy all their enquiries with respect to our Selves and the Object of our pursute."[7]

In early May, the travelers were back among the Nez Perce, at a village near where the Clearwater River flows into the Snake, and Sacagawea was again called on to translate. This time the intermediary was a Shoshone man who was a prisoner of the Nez Perce. Again the translation chain was tedious, and it took the captains several hours to tell the Indians what they wanted.[8]

What the Nez Perce were saying was clear: It would be weeks before the snows of the Bitterroots would permit the Americans to continue their journey. They had been too impatient to start home. Now they must play a waiting game. After the momentous trip west, it must have been exasperating. For Toussaint, it meant repeated errands to buy camas roots that the Nez Perce dug on the Weippe Prairie. "These roots are a good diet, but in general we do not relish them as well as meat," Gass observed. In addition to complaints concerning the food, there were constant laments about the weather. "We had a cloudy wet morning . . . We again had a very wet morning . . . In the evening there were some light showers."[9]

At times, there was excitement enough and to spare. As Toussaint and Lepage made their way up the Clearwater to swap for roots at a village eight miles from camp, their pack horse slipped on the side of a steep cliff and fell into the river. The panicky horse swam across the stream, and an Indian on the far shore tried to drive it back. The pack cinches broke, and the horse's load of valuable trade goods, including a dressed elk skin, went overboard. The Indians, hearing the two traders were coming, tried to cross the river with a raft piled with roots and bread. The raft struck a rock and capsized, and Toussaint and Lepage returned empty handed.[10]

On May 22, Toussaint faced a worry more serious than the loss of trade goods. His son, Jean Baptiste, was very ill. For several days, the fifteen-month-old had been suffering from diarrhea. The child was cutting teeth, but it soon became evident this was more than a teething problem. The diarrhea abated, but Baptiste was running a high fever and his neck and throat were badly swollen. Some commentators have speculated that the child had mumps, others that he had tonsillitis and an infected cervical lymph gland, or perhaps an abscess on his neck, or mastoiditis. The captains feared he was near death. For eighteen straight days, each of them mentioned his condition in their journals.[11]

On May 23, the baby was reported to be somewhat better. After applications of a wild onion poultice, the swelling did not seem to have increased. The next day, Lewis was more concerned. Baptiste had spent a restless night, and the swelling in his jaw and the back of his neck had increased. Lewis supplemented the onion poultice with doses of cream of tartar. On May 25, Gass believed the child was getting better. Next day, Clark found him "not so well today as yesterday." That evening, Lewis gave Baptiste an enema, probably of warm water, either plain or soapy. After another night, the swelling was down, and the fever had passed. On May 27, at last, Lewis was able to report that Toussaint's son was much better although he might be left with a disfiguring mark below his ear. On June 3, the captains reported their young patient almost well. Two days later, Clark applied a salve of pine resin, beeswax, and bear oil, which he believed cleared up the inflammation, although there was a hard lump under the child's left ear.[12] The Nez Perce were telling them that if they attempted the Bitterroots before July 1, their horses would face at least three days without food at the summit. But Lewis wanted to get going as soon as possible, and began preparations for a mid-June departure. On June 7, Toussaint and four others rode in a light snowfall to an Indian village to trade fishing gear, old pieces of iron, bullets, and other odds and ends for the ropes and strings they would need to lash their loads. When Toussaint and Hugh McNeal returned, each had procured only one string.[13]

The Corps of Discovery set out at eleven o'clock on the morning of June 10, feeling ready for the Bitterroots. Their plan was to rest for a few days among the pale blue blossoms of the camas fields on Weippe Prairie and lay in a supply of meat. After that, Clark reckoned, "the Snows will have melted more off the mountains and the grass raised to a sufficient hight for our horses to live." He was wrong. They soon found that without guides they would never find their way through the deep snow. Two days into their journey, they cached many of their goods in trees and, for the first time since the expedition began, turned back. It was a wise decision. On June 24, they set out again and made it across the mountains to their old camp at Traveler's Rest, near present-day Missoula, in six days. On the way west, it had taken them eleven days of hard marching.[14]

At eight A.M. on July 3, the commanders split up for the longest time they would be apart during the entire expedition Lewis selected six men to go north with him to investigate the Marias. Toussaint and Sacagawea, with Baptiste, went with Clark to explore the Yellowstone. They could be invaluable to Clark as interpreters should they meet Crow Indians, whose language was similar to that of the Hidatsas. The couple's absence would, however, leave Lewis with no one to translate from the Shoshone tongue.[15]

Now, Sacagawea made one of her rare contributions as a guide. Clark was thinking of going some twenty miles out of his way to reach the Yellowstone by way of Flathead Pass to the north. Sacagawea, familiar with the country from her childhood, pointed out that they could save time by going through the more southerly Bozeman Pass. Clark gratefully took her advice and implied it was not the first time she had "been of great Service to me as a pilot through this Country." Two days later, with their horses limping on the rocky terrain, they reached the Yellowstone as it flowed majestically from between the Gallatin Range and the Absaroka Range.[16]

The Clark party found itself beset with accidents. On July 18, near White Beaver Creek in what is now South Central Montana, Toussaint galloped off in pursuit of a buffalo. His horse stepped into a badger hole and he was thrown over the mount's head. His hip, shoulder, and face were bruised. [17]

A more serious mishap befell Private George Gibson. Gibson, one of the better horsemen on the expedition, fell from his steed while attempting to mount after shooting a deer. His fall sent an inch-thick burnt snag nearly two inches into his thigh. With Gibson unable to ride, Clark set his men to building canoes for them and their baggage so they could continue their journey by water.[18]

At eleven A.M. on July 18, Clark saw smoke rising from plains to the southeast. He assumed it was a signal, perhaps warning other tribes of strangers. The next day, while Clark was walking in the woods, Toussaint spotted an Indian on a bluff across the river. Clark saw smoke rising again. This time it seemed to be in the snow-covered mountains.[19]

When he awoke on July 21, Clark was greeted by the news that twenty-four of his fifty horses were missing. As so often, he turned to Toussaint. While the trusted interpreter searched upstream, George Shannon was sent downstream and William Bratton scoured the low lands near their camp. They found no horses, but the sturdy Bratton, after a day-long search, returned to say there was a large Indian lodge about twelve miles away. If they could not find horses, thought Clark, perhaps they could find tracks. Toussaint and Nathaniel Pryor searched the next morning, but found neither. The perplexed commander's next plan was for Toussaint, Pryor, Shannon and Bratton to encircle the camp, find the tracks and pursue the horses. They looked all evening, but still found no tracks. The plains were dry and hard, and tracks difficult to see. But why would horses leave grassy river bottoms and take off over dry plains? Clark thought he knew the answer: the Indians had taken the horses over the plains to prevent their being followed.[20]

Clark figured Labiche, a skilled tracker whose mother was an Omaha Indian, could find the horses' route if anybody could. He sent him out early in the morning on a large circle around the camp. Labiche saw what the others could not: the tracks of horses making off into the open plains, going very fast.[21]

The next day, from his canoe, Clark saw the lodge Shannon told him about. Expecting to find Crow Indians, he prepared a lecture telling them he had "looked in every derection for you, without seeing you untill now." In an unusual flight of fancy for him, he said his horses had complained to him that their comrades had been taken away by the Crows. Addressing the Indians as "Children," as he and Lewis did throughout the expedition, he said that their "Great Father the chief of all the white people" would be sorry to hear of their thievery. Toussaint never did get to interpret this for the Crows, because Clark's party did not find them or recover the horses.[22]

Clark sent the rest of the animals and baggage with Pryor, ordering him to take them overland to the Mandan villages while he and the rest of the party proceeded by water. On Pryor's second night on the trail, the rest of the horses were stolen. He and his men sewed buffalo skins together, made them watertight, and stretched them over willow poles to make bull boats, a staple of American Indian navigation, so they could catch up with Clark.[23]

On his way downstream , Clark walked 250 paces from the river to explore a sandstone outcropping 200 feet high. Most of its sides were cliffs too steep to climb, but there was one way up it. When he reached the top, Clark found two piles of stone on which Indians had carved animals. He added his own inscription, "Wm Clark July 25 1805" and named the outcropping "Pompys Tower" in honor of little Jean Baptiste Charbonneau. His early journal editor Nicholas Biddle changed the name of the rock formation to the more classical "Pompey's Pillar," the name of a granite column in Alexandria honoring the Roman general who was killed in Egypt after challenging Julius Caesar's power. Today Clark's words, protected by shatterproof glass, can be read on the hilltop near Billings, Montana.[24]

Mosquitoes were keeping the travelers awake at night. By the time they reached the Missouri River on August 7 in two small canoes lashed together, Baptiste's face was puffed up by the insects' bites. Clark had agreed to wait for Lewis at the confluence of the two rivers, but now he changed plans. He and his party

Pompey's Pillar, east of Billings, Montana, named by William Clark in honor of "my little dancing boy Baptiest," whom he called Pomp. (Photo by Joyce Miller Nelson)

William Clark carved his name and the date into the sandstone of Pompey's Pillar. Today, it is protected by bulletproof glass and can still be read by visitors. (Photo by Joyce Miller Nelson)

were tired and wanted to escape the mosquitoes, so he left a note on a pole telling his co-commander that they were going on downstream.[25]

Lewis overtook them on August 12, and they camped near the creek they had named for Charbonneau. At the Mandan villages two days later, they sent their interpreter to ask the chief to visit. At a carefully selected level spot on the river bank, Clark invited the chiefs to come to Washington to meet with President Jefferson. He was told that Little Crow, the second chief of the Mandans, wanted to accept. When Clark and Toussaint walked to the village to see when Little Crow would be ready, the chief told them he still wanted to go, but wished to talk to his people first. After this meeting, he said he had changed his mind. The principal chief, Big White, was jealous of the attention his subordinate was getting, and the two had argued. Big White said he would go to Washington himself if he could take his wife and son. The captains felt obliged to agree.[26]

Toussaint had been renewing old acquaintances in Metaharta, and he brought disturbing news. Despite the commanders' peace-making efforts, the Hidatsas had been sending war parties to fight the Shoshones and the Arikaras. Clark took the expedition's small cannon, which they had no further use for, to the lodge of the one-eyed Hidatsa chief Le Borgne. Gathering the chiefs around the cannon in a circle, he reproached them for killing "pore defenceless" Shoshones when "our backs were Scercely turned." With the gun as bait, he tried to persuade the Hidatsas to come meet with their "white father" in Washington. The Indians "appeared very fond" of the gun, but declined the invitation. They were afraid, they said, of the warlike Sioux below them on the river.[27]

On August 17, the Corps loaded up for the final leg to St. Louis. With no chiefs for whom to interpret, Toussaint said he would stay with the Mandan people. He would have been glad to come if the chiefs of his villages had agreed, but as it was there would be nothing for him to do. Clark had another idea: Why didn't he come anyway and find a new life in Illinois or somewhere? No, said Toussaint, "he had no acquaintance or prospects of makeing a living below , and must continue to live the way he had done." Clark offered to take his and Sacagawea's "butifull promising child," now nineteen months old. But Baptiste was not yet weaned. When the boy was a year older, his parents said, Toussaint would take him to Clark, who promised to raise him "in such a manner as I thought proper." So it was settled. Toussaint was paid $500.33 and one-third cents—the $409.16 and two-thirds cents he was due in salary plus the price of a horse and lodge. The captains also gave him the Corps of Discovery's valuable bellows and blacksmith's tools, "supposing they might be useful" to the Mandans and Hidatsas.[28]

It was in a roster designed to show which members of the Corps might deserve extra pay that Lewis made his famous evaluation of Charbonneau as a "man of no peculiar merit" who nonetheless was valuable as an interpreter "from the moment of our departure from the Mandans, on the 7th of April 1805 until our return to that place in August last." He made no mention of Sacagawea or their child. Of Drouillard, the Corps' other interpreter, he said: "A man of much merit; he has been peculiarly useful from his knowledge of the common language of gesticulation, and his uncommon skill as a hunter and woodsman; those several duties he performed in good faith, and with an ardor which deserves the highest commendation." His appraisal of Toussaint, while less generous than his words about Drouillard, was fair. He did not think him outstanding in his discharge of other duties, but had found him a useful, honorable and hard working interpreter. [29]

Clark was so busy with last-minute preparations for departure that he had little time to talk to his friend Toussaint. On board the pirogue bound for St. Louis, however, he found that time. As the boat drifted past the mouth of the Cannonball River near the present North-South Dakota border, he wrote a letter and sent it to Toussaint by one of the fur traders they met coming up the Missouri. "You have been a long time with me," he wrote, "and have conducted your Self in such a manner as to gain my friendship, your woman who accompanied you that long dangerous and fatiguing rout to the Pacific Ocian and back diserved a greater reward for her attention and services on that rout than we had in our power to give her at the Mandans. As to your little Son (my boy Pomp) you well know my fondness for him."[30]

"Your present situation with the Indians gives me some concern," he said. Again, he urged Toussaint to "come on with me to the Illinois where it most probably would be in my power to put you in some way to do something for your self." He repeated, "that you may be certain of it" of his promise to raise Baptiste.[31]

"Charbono, if you wish to live with the white people, and will come to me I will give you a piece of land and furnish you with horses cows and hogs," the captain wrote. He recognized that Toussaint still had friends in Montreal. If he wished to visit them, "I will let you have a horse, and your family will be taken care of untill your return."[32]

The Army would be sending troops to the Mandan villages to protect the American fur trade, and if Toussaint wished to go along as an interpreter, Clark would see that he was hired. On the other hand, if the long-time fur trader wanted to return to his old occupation and would leave Baptiste with Clark, the captain would help him with trade merchandise. He would even be willing to join him in the business on a small scale, sending a boat load of goods at a time into Indian territory under his charge.[33]

If he accepted either offer and would bring Baptiste, he said, "Janey [Sacagawaea] had best come along with you to take care of the boy untill I get him." He advised Toussaint to hang on to his pay and whatever furs and buffalo robes he had. He urged him to try to get more, especially the skins of big horn sheep and pronghorn, so he could bring them to St. Louis in the spring. At the governor's office, there would be a letter from Clark waiting for him, telling him how best to dispose of the furs and robes and where to find him.[34]

He asked Toussaint to let him know if he did not intend to come. He signed his name as "Your Friend William Clark," expressing "anxious expectations of seeing my little danceing boy Baptiest." The reference to the two-year-old as a "danceing boy" is intriguing. Did the child perhaps prance to Cruzatte's campfire fiddling?[35]

In a postscript, Clark advised Toussaint to show the letter to only one or two persons, presumably the one or two who would read it to him and write down his reply. "When you write to me seal your letter," he said.[36]

Perhaps Toussaint responded to this extraordinary act of generosity. If so, his reply has been lost. He did go to St. Louis, but not to stay. Toussaint Charbonneau would remain with the Indians whom he had known for so long.[37]

Afterward

T he St. Louis to which the Lewis and Clark party returned was much changed from the frontier village they had visited on their way to the Mandan Villages in 1803. Then a scattering of houses made of mud, stone and rough-hewn logs had been crammed onto three streets at the river's edge. Now the village had grown into a city with a population of about 5,000. Before, dead animals had rotted where they fell; now, there was an ordinance requiring their removal. There were speed limits for horses and carts. The town was thinking of starting a public library.[1]

Among St. Louis's citizens by the end of 1809 were Toussaint, Sacagawea, and their son Jean Baptiste. They had indicated to Clark they would bring the child to him two years earlier, but may have delayed because hostile Arikara Indians were making river travel dangerous below the Mandan villages. Or maybe they just could not afford a trip to the city. In 1807, however, Toussaint had received another $409.16 and two-thirds cents under a bill passed by Congress doubling the explorers' pay. The bill also granted each of them a parcel of land west of the Mississippi. Clark signed for the 320 acres granted to Toussaint, but it is not known whether Toussaint ever took possession of the acreage.[2]

Whatever was responsible for their timing, they were there in 1809, and were attending to something that the Roman Catholic Toussaint clearly thought important—the baptism of his son.

The new boom town was not a very religious community. Father Joseph Marie Dumand, a Trappist prior, had visited the city from Kentucky just a year before and bewailed the "irreligion and licentiousness [that] had made their way into this distant land." Toussaint, however, made sure that his nearly five-year-old boy would have the benefits of the sacrament of baptism.

St. Louis had no resident Catholic priest, but Father Urban Guillet, a Trappist from a monastery across the frozen Mississippi River and twenty miles to the east, was in town for the Christmas season. On December 28, Toussaint and Sacagawea stood by as the white-robed monk made the sign of the cross with holy water on Baptiste's forehead and intoned in French, "I baptize thee in the name of the Father, the Son, and the Holy Ghost."

Neither Lewis nor Clark was present at the ceremony in the small vertical-log church. Lewis had died of a gunshot wound, probably suicide although some thought it murder, at an inn on the Natchez Trace on October 11 of that year. Clark was in Washington on business. But Auguste Chouteau, a friend of Clark and a co-founder of St. Louis, signed the baptismal certificate as godfather, after Father Guillet's signature. Chouteau's twelve-year-old daughter, Eulalie, signed her name just below his. Then Toussaint made his "X" as "pere de l'enfant." He was described in the document as "living in this parish."[3]

In 1810 Toussaint was still in St. Louis, providing information for Clark to use in answering queries from Nicholas Biddle, who was preparing the first edition of the Lewis and Clark journals.

Clark relied on Toussaint, "the Interpreter who is now with me," for knowledge of American Indians.[4]

Clark suggested to Toussaint that he might want to take up farming, and on October 30, 1810, the interpreter bought land on the Missouri in St. Ferdinand Township near St. Louis from his former commander. Toussaint was no farmer, however. On March 26, 1811, he sold the land back to Clark for $100. Francois Robidou, a mutual friend of the two men, witnessed the deed. Toussaint bought fifty pounds of hardtack from August Chouteau and signed to embark on a keelboat voyage up the Missouri. Sacagawea was with him. He had hired on as an interpreter for Manuel Lisa, who had spent the winter of 1808-1809 organizing the Missouri Fur Company.[5]

Being on Manuel Lisa's crew was a wise move for anybody who wanted to get back into the fur trade. The brash, headstrong Spanish-American had moved from New Orleans to St. Louis while still in his teens. Before his nineteenth birthday, his aggressive bargaining had won him a grant of exclusive trade with the Osage Indians. In 1807, he went up the Missouri and built the trading post of Fort Manuel where the Bighorn River flows into the Yellowstone, between present Billings and Miles City, Montana.[6]

The country along the Missouri River to which Toussaint Charbonneau returned was a far cry from the country he had left for the unknown West. No longer would the North West Company and Hudson's Bay Company divide the fur trade with the Indians between them. Even as Lewis and Clark made their way back down the Missouri, they had met American fur hunters eager for the treasures that had been unlocked.

In New York, John Jacob Astor was one of the first to feel the ground shifting. On a four-month voyage from London to Baltimore in the winter of 1783-84, while Hudson's Bay nabobs strolled the decks of the ship *North Carolina* over his head, the twenty-year-old Astor had listened as a fellow steerage passenger, returning from selling his furs in English markets, outlined the glowing profits to be reaped in his trade. Astor was hooked, and his foresight would make him the richest man in America. Others would follow his lead, struggling to compete for the estimated six million pelts that were sold each year. Now, with Toussaint often at his side, Lisa would make his Missouri Fur Company a rival to Astor in cutthroat competition for furs.[7]

Lisa talked the Pittsburgh lawyer and journalist Henry Brackenridge into joining his twenty-man expedition as a hunter. In his journal, Brackenridge described Sacagawea as "a good creature, of a mild and gentle disposition, greatly attracted to the whites, whose manners and dress she tries to imitate." But she had become sickly, he said, "and longed to revisit her native country." Toussaint too, wrote Brackenridge, "had become weary of a civilized life."[8]

The trip was Lisa's third up the Missouri. It sprang from his touchy relationship with Astor, who had founded the American Fur Company in 1808 and the Pacific Fur Company soon afterward. Astor's idea was to establish transportation routes on the Mississippi and build "a range of Posts or trading houses on the rout made by Captn Lewis to the Sea." In furtherance of this, he sent an expedition headed by his partner, the New Jersey entrepreneur Wilson Price Hunt, up the Missouri by boat with instructions to cut across to the Pacific by land and look for likely locations. Lisa embarked from St. Louis with the aim of overtaking Hunt and combining forces with him.[9]

Although nominally an interpreter, Toussaint was entrusted by Lisa with other missions. On April 11 1811, he and Brackenridge were sent to make inquiries on shore below the mouth of the Osage River. They were told that Hunt had passed there three weeks before. Lisa put on speed, and by May 19 learned that Hunt was only four days ahead of him. He sent Toussaint to ask Astor's partner to wait. Toussaint returned a week later saying Hunt had promised to delay at a Ponca Indian village near Bon Homme Island in present South Dakota. The barge reached the village the same day, but Lisa found that Hunt had left three days before.[10]

Lisa raced ahead and overtook the elusive Hunt on June 2, but they quarreled, and it was agreed that Hunt would trade his boats for horses at Lisa's North Dakota fort. From the Mandan villages, the Hunt party proceeded overland to the Pacific, as directed by Astor. Lisa returned to St. Louis, leaving Toussaint behind as an interpreter at a post he had established near the site of Lewis and Clark's Fort Mandan.[11]

When Congress declared war on Britain on June 18, 1812, Lisa was on the Missouri again, busy establishing another fur trading post. The chief cause of the War of 1812 was British interference with U.S. shipping, but President James Madison also mentioned the hostility to Americans of Indian tribes "in constant intercourse with British traders and garrisons." Clark, by now superintendent of Indian affairs at St. Louis and a major stockholder in the Missouri Fur Company, as well as its president, commissioned Lisa as a sub-agent to keep the Missouri River Indians at peace with the United States.[12]

In August, 1812, Lisa built a second Fort Manuel, seventy miles south of present Bismark, North Dakota, and hired John C. Luttig, a St. Louis trader with a reputation for hard work and hard drinking, to be its chief clerk. Luttig took a dim view of Toussaint and his fellow interpreter, Rene Jusseaume. "These two rascals ought to be hung for their perfidy," he said, "they do more harm than good to the American government, stir up the Indians and pretend to be friends to the white People at the same time but we find them to be our Ennemies." He gleefully quoted an Indian woman as saying that "C. & J. were Lyars and not to be considered as good french men." Men on these expeditions were frequently suspicious of interpreters who were on good terms with the Indians and could talk with them in languages trappers did not understand. But whatever prejudice Luttig may have harbored against French-Indian interpreters, the record does not justify his rancor.[13]

Toussaint was certainly excitable. On a windy September day, a party of men including the hunter and trapper Francois Lecompte went out from the fort to retrieve seven stray horses. They spotted the animals but before they could recover them a group of Indians mounted them and rode off. Toussaint dashed into the fort on horseback crying out "To Arms Lecompte is Killed." As Luttig told the story, the Indians had actually only told Lecompte to "go about his business." As for Toussaint, said Luttig, "he run off and left the poor fellow . . . if the Indians had an Idea to Kill him they might easy have done it." A few days later, Toussaint and Jusseaume recovered three of the horses.[14]

On November 15, after receiving a report that the Arikaras were planning to make war on his post, Lisa sent Toussaint and two others to try for an amicable settlement. That night, word came back that the Arikaras promised to return horses they had stolen and "requested Mr. M. L. to be tranquil, Matters would be settled." On the 17th, the Indians returned two horses, and a council was held with them that "finished with Peace." Luttig's view notwithstanding, Toussaint was proving a trusted and valuable employee.[15]

On December 20, a "clear and moderate" Sunday, Luttig recorded that "this Evening the wife of Charbonneau a Snake Squaw, died of a putrid fever." He did not name the dead woman, but described her as about twenty-five years old, as Sacagawea would have been at the time. She was, said Luttig, "a good woman—the best in the fort." He said she left "a fine infant girl," born the previous summer. The child, named Lisette, was about four months old.[16] An alternative theory of Sacagawea's life and death is discussed in the epilogue to this book.

As the winter of 1812-13 deepened, the trading for furs was deteriorating. On February 21, the coldest day yet, Toussaint traveled to the Mandan villages and obtained only one hundred and sixty-eight out of a possible four hundred and ninety-two skins. On the way back to Fort Manuel, he passed a band of Cheyenne Indians who warned him his life was in danger. They said they had spotted twenty-seven men—Sioux warriors, they believed—nearby. Toussaint arrived safely at the fort, but brought ominous news. Men from the North West Company had visited the Hidatsas in December promising to "furnish them with every thing without Pay if they would go to war, and rob and Kill the Americans . . . thus are those Bloodhounds the British constantly employed."[17]

The next day, one of Lisa's hunters, Louis Archambeau, ventured outside the fort to haul a sleigh load of hay. He was killed and scalped. The men saw Arikara, Mandan and Cheyenne Indians encamped around them. The inhabitants of the fort were, said Luttig, "like Prisoners in Deserts to expect every moment our fate." Guard was maintained constantly. Dogs were sent outside to give the alarm in case of impending attack. On the clear, cold evening of March 1, Toussaint set off to return to the Mandan villages, escorted by five armed men from the fort. His escorts returned two days later, saying the Arikaras were on their way to trade. The Indians did not show up. On March 5, in the midst of a snowstorm, Luttig made the last entry in his journal. It simply said that four Mandans who had arrived the day before, on their way to the Arikaras, had resumed their route.[18]

What happened afterward is unclear. Christian Wilt, a merchant who worked for Lisa, said the Americans abandoned the post after an attack in which the Sioux killed fifteen of Lisa's men. Other accounts said the post was burned. Apparently, Lisa headed down the Missouri with his forty packs of beaver pelts and 300 packs of buffalo hides, and with Lisette Charbonneau, the baby born to Toussaint and Sacagawea four months before her death. Lisa arrived in St. Louis on June 1 and relayed Toussaint's report that the North West Company had been inciting the Indians to enter the war. After the attack on Fort Manuel, Toussaint disappeared. According to one unconfirmed account, he was captured by the British and taken to Canada as a prisoner.[19]

On August, 11, 1813, Luttig asked the Orphan's Court at St. Louis to appoint him guardian of the children of Toussaint Charbonneau. He listed Toussaint as deceased, apparently believing he had been killed in the attack on Fort Manuel. The children were listed as Toussaint, a boy about ten, and a girl, Lisette, about one year old. There is no mention of Baptiste, who would have been eight, and there is no other record of a son named Toussaint. Luttig most likely got the names mixed up and guessed a couple of years wrong on the boy's age.

About this time, Luttig went to work for Clark. Shortly afterward, his name was crossed out on the document, and that of Clark substituted.[20]

Toussaint was in St. Louis again by July, 1816, and signed on as a member of an ill-fated trading venture. Pierre Chouteau, whose hospitality Meriwether Lewis had enjoyed a dozen years before during his stop-over in St. Louis, was retiring from the fur business. One of his son Auguste's first priorities was to establish the Chouteau name on the upper Arkansas River (now in Colorado but then on the border between the United States and Mexico). Mexican authorities charged young Chouteau, his partner Jules de Mun and nineteen others with trading illegally in Spanish territory and they spent forty-eight days in a Santa Fe prison, some of them in chains. Their ordeal gave rise to another story about Toussaint being imprisoned. However, depositions the men made after returning to St. Louis make it appear more likely he was in a group sent back in charge of lame horses before the arrests occurred.[21]

Toussaint was once again in the city where his son, Baptiste, had been growing to manhood.

Father and Son

On January 20, 1820, William Clark, superintendent of Indian affairs at St. Louis, paid $16.37 and one-half cents to J. E. Welch, a Baptist minister and school teacher, to cover tuition, ink, and firewood for two quarters for Jean Baptiste Charbonneau.[1]

Clark was making good on his offer to educate the "butifull promising Child" he had grown fond of during their two-year expedition to the Pacific Ocean.[2]

More payments by Clark for Baptiste's education are recorded throughout 1820. On March 31, there is a payment to L. T. Honore' for boarding, lodging, and washing the boy during the first quarter of the year. On April 1, storekeepers J. and G. H. Kennerly are paid $1.50 each for a Roman history, a dictionary and a lesson book, another $1.50 for two dozen sheets of paper and a supply of quill pens, $1.00 for a ciphering book, and sixty-two cents for a slate and pencils. They also were paid $17.75 for shoes, socks, a hat, and four yards of cloth.

Welch, who boarded Indian and half-Indian boys, was paid

another $8.37 and one-half cents for an additional quarter's tuition, including fuel and ink. The Reverend Francis Neil, a Roman Catholic priest who conducted a boarding school that later became St. Louis University, was paid twelve dollars on May 17 for one quarter's tuition for a half-Indian boy identified as Toussaint Charbonneau. This might have been the mysterious other son, but it is more likely that the father's name was used by mistake instead of the child's. On June 30 and again on October 1, Honore received forty-five dollars for board, lodging, and washing of Baptiste, in each case for three months. These expenditures were listed in official papers as "expenditures by Capt. W. Clark as superintendent of Indian affairs" at St., Louis, raising the unanswered question of whether he was paying out of his own pocket or the government was footing the bill.[3]

Baptiste apparently spent school vacations at the elder Charbonneau's home among the Mandans. A white trader reported seeing him there at the age of eleven or twelve, speaking fluent French, and told a perhaps apocryphal tale of the boy's gift horse being gambled away by his father.[4]

By this time, Toussaint Charbonneau was a government interpreter based at Council Bluffs but ranging widely throughout the Missouri River country. From 1819 until 1839, he was employed by every United States Indian agent and sub-agent for the Mandan and Upper Missouri tribes. His salaries ranged from $200 to $400 a year. Even the lower figure was equal to the amount generally paid a sub-agent.

Sometimes, Toussaint earned extra money for running errands. In August, 1825, he delivered presents to the Hidatsas at Metaharta and carried blankets and other goods to a government agent. For each trip, he was paid ten dollars. The agent, in one of the more unusual of the many phonetic spellings of Toussaint's name, made out a receipt for "Tusan Shabbonow" to sign with his "X."[5]

Toussaint must have picked up at least a smattering of English from the American traders he dealt with. None of them mentioned the kind of complicated translation chain that plagued Lewis and Clark. He also apparently broadened his knowledge of Indian languages. Fur trader David Meriwether, who employed him as an interpreter, said he "spoke the language, I believe, of every Indian tribe on the Missouri from the Rocky Mountains to its mouth."[6]

In 1819 and 1820, Toussaint was an interpreter for army engineer Stephen Harriman Long's expedition to the Rocky Mountains, which yielded valuable topographical information about the West. As often was the case, the interpreter was sometimes more conciliatory to the Indians than were others on the expedition. Once, a Pawnee backed up by several members of the tribe was seen carrying off a package of pounded meat. One of the officers wrestled the meat away from the Indians, and there was talk of punishment. But the Pawnees were permitted to keep the meat after Toussaint said it was his and he had given it to them.[7]

Toussaint was also interpreting in the summer of 1823 when Colonel Henry Leavenworth of Fort Atkinson, north of present Omaha, made a rash foray up the Missouri to punish the Arikaras for a series of raids that had killed twenty-five traders. When Leavenworth arrived at the Arikara villages on August 8 with his band of 220 soldiers, eighty mountain men and more than 400 Sioux Indians, he barged into a parley between an Arikara and a Sioux.[8]

With Toussaint interpreting, the Arikara told Leavenworth "that we had killed the man who had done all the mischief and who had caused both us and themselves so much trouble." The Arikara asked Leavenworth to "permit the Chiefs to come out immediately to speak to us, and that we would meet them and tell them on what terms we would make peace."

The Arikaras were willing to fight the Sioux, but went back into their village when they saw the soldiers. Leavenworth bombarded the village to little effect with two six-pounders and a howitzer. He planned an attack, but gave it up when the Sioux would not join in. The Arikaras agreed to return property they had stolen from a fur company camp, but turned over only three guns, one horse and sixteen robes before running away.

On August 14, the colonel sent Toussaint and an escort to look for the Arikaras, bearing a note: "Ricaras you see the pipe of peace which you gave to me in the hands of Mr. Charbonneau and the flag of the United States. These will convince you that my heart is not bad—your villages are in my possession. Come back and take them in peace and you will find everything as you left them, you shall not be hurt if you do not obstruct the road or molest the traders—if you do not come back there are some bad men and bad Indians who will burn your villages. Come back and come quickly. Be assured that what I say is the truth."

Toussaint's mission failed to salvage Leavenworth's ill-conceived venture. The party found no sign of Indians, and the colonel returned down the river.[9]

Meanwhile, the younger Charbonneau's education was about to take a dramatic turn.

At Home and Abroad

On June 21, 1823, Duke Paul Wilhelm Freidrich Herzog, of Wurttemberg, a scholarly German nobleman exploring the "vast, silent places" of North America, disembarked at a trading settlement where the Kansas River flows into the Missouri.

Among the traders he met there was Jean Baptiste Charbonneau.

It was the beginning of an odyssey that would introduce the young frontiersman to the courts of Europe and help shape the rest of his life.[1]

The duke, a nephew of Wurttemberg's King Friedrich I, had been trained for a military career. But like Thomas Jefferson, the impulsive, intellectual Paul was more interested in science and philosophy than in soldiering, and professed to prefer the wilds to a royal court. "In the atmosphere of a palace I would feel like a wild thing that is imprisoned in a gilded cage," he said. "My heart would never cease to hunger for the vast, silent places."[2]

Resigning his commission, he studied botany and zoology and set his sights on the New World. After securing permission from

Chalk drawing of Baptiste Charbonneau's patron, Duke Paul Wilhelm of Wurttemberg. "In the atmosphere of a palace . . . my heart would never cease to hunger for the vast silent spaces." (Courtesy Stadt Bad Mergentheim and Deuschordensmuseum Bad Mergentheim, Germany)

Secretary of State John Quincy Adams to visit the United States, he set sail from Hamburg for New Orleans. From there he made his way to St. Louis where William Clark, as a representative of the War Department, approved his plan to follow the Lewis and Clark route up the Missouri to the Mandan villages. Visiting seventy-three-year-old Auguste Chouteau at his home at nearby Florissant, he arranged for passage upriver on a "Messrs. Chouteaus & Co. Boat." [3]

When they reached the Kansas River settlement, where Kansas City, Kansas, now stands, the duke learned Baptiste's history before proceeding upstream. [4]

By a quirk of fate, Duke Paul found Baptiste's father waiting for him when he arrived three weeks later at Fort Recovery, ten miles north of the White River. Toussaint brought an invitation for him to visit Fort Kiowa, twenty miles farther upstream. During their visit, the duke no doubt told Toussaint Charbonneau of meeting his son. Toussaint had been working with traders at Fort Kiowa, but also did some interpreting for Duke Paul. When Paul arrived back in St. Louis in the fall of 1823, Baptiste was with him. The two young men had hit it off. Baptiste was now eighteen, and the duke was only twenty-five. No doubt they talked to each other in French. It was the language of Baptiste's father and of the St. Louis schools he had attended, as well as the language of the courts in which the duke had grown up.[5]

The two sailed from St. Louis December 23 on the steamboat Cincinnati for New Orleans. There they found the copper-bottomed brig Smyrna tied up near a water works, and booked passage for Europe. But the three-masted ship was becalmed for three weeks before setting out in sunny weather. It was the first time Baptiste had crossed a body of water broader than the Missouri River. In Germany, the duke employed him as a hunter on the grounds of his castle in the woods about thirty miles from Stuttgart, and sent him to Wurttemberg's obligatory public schools.[6]

Duke Paul also took Baptiste with him on travels in Germany, England, France, and North Africa. But in 1827, the duke married and evidently decided it was time for the young American to go home. Two years later, when Duke Paul embarked on the second of his five trips to America, he again obtained Clark's approval for a trip up the Missouri and set out from St. Louis with "two hired men of the American Fur Company." Baptiste may have been one of them, it is not known, but it is certain that he was back in his homeland to stay.[7]

He had obviously gained some polish from his years in Europe, and he took it with him into the Far West. Connecticut-born journalist Rufus Sage, encountering him on an island in the South Platte River, said the youth "had acquired a classic education and could converse fluently in German, Spanish, French and English, as well as several Indian languages."

Clark's "little Danceing boy" had grown, said Sage, into "a gentleman of superior education" with "a quaint humor and shrewdness in his conversation. "[8]

About the time his son set sail for Europe, Toussaint embarked from the Mandan villages for a canoe trip on the Missouri. With him were five men of the fur trading firm of Bernard Pratte & Company, a newcomer to the trade closely allied to the Chouteaus of St. Louis. Toussaint was worried, because before leaving he had met with Indians at the villages and warned Joseph Brazeau, the Bernard Pratte clerk, that the men would be slaughtered by Arikaras. Apparently, the warning was not heeded. When the canoe came within a day's march of an Arikara village, Toussaint got out "and went by land, knowing there was less danger than by water." The next morning, he heard from Indians that the five men had been killed.[9]

The aftermath of Leavenworth's foray was still souring relations with the Missouri River tribes and Congress responded by authorizing a good will expedition. President John Quincy Adams appointed General Henry Atkinson as Army commander. Benjamin O'Fallon, a troublesome, hot-tempered nephew whom William Clark had helped to get a job in the Indian Department, was chosen as the department's representative. On May 25, 1825, nine keelboats, four-hundred-and-seventy six soldiers, and forty horses left Fort Atkinson.[10]

The emissaries staged parades, fired off rockets, handed out presents, and signed sixteen treaties. The eleventh, with the Arikaras, was signed at one P.M. on July 30 at the lower Mandan village, near where Lewis and Clark, Toussaint, and Sacagawea had wintered together twenty years before, and where Jean Baptiste had been born.[11]

The Mandans contended the attacks on American fur traders had been the work of hot-headed young warriors who thought the traders were hostile Indians. The government accepted the explanation and the Mandans acknowledged the supremacy of the United States over them. They promised to trade only with Americans. Both parties pledged a "firm and lasting peace."[12]

After Atkinson, O'Fallon and an array of Mandan chiefs and warriors signed, twenty-eight representatives of the United States—army officers, Indian agents and others—signed as witnesses. The last, making his "X", was the interpreter, Toussaint Charbonneau.[13]

The Prince and the Frontiersman

The sloppily dressed bachelor with bad teeth and a heavy German accent stood on the deck of the Missouri River steamboat *Assiniboine* and watched the Stars and Stripes waving from the flag staff of Fort Clark, the American Fur Company post below the Mandan villages. It was June 18, 1833, and Alexander Philip Maximilian, Prince of Wied-Neuwied, was about to make the acquaintance of Toussaint Charbonneau.[1]

Their partnership would be fortunate. As an educated European, the prince certainly knew French. Toussaint, as an interpreter of American Indian languages, could help him with the Indian studies that had brought him to America. He was also better acquainted with the country's wildlife. The prince had seen his first cottonwood tree in Portsmouth, Ohio, his first yellow-headed blackbird near Leavenworth, Kansas, his first bison in the land that is now South Dakota.[2]

The two were unlikely companions. When Toussaint returned home with Lewis and Clark in August of 1806, Maximilian was fighting in the Prussian army that would be crushed by Napoleon at Jena two months later. Nine years later, he was a major-general in the army of allies that entered Paris in triumph after Napoleon's defeat at Waterloo.[3]

But like Baptiste's benefactor Duke Paul, Maximilian was more interested in botany, zoology and native peoples than in a military career. Before coming to America, he had established his scientific reputation with two years of field work in South America and the study of natural history.[4]

The prince had arrived in Boston on July 4, 1832, eager to explore North America. Making his way to St. Louis, he embarked up the Missouri on the *Yellowstone*, the first of the steam-driven sidewheelers Manuel Lisa had introduced on the river, signaling that the keelboat era was nearing its end. When the *Yellowstone* turned back with a load of furs, Maximilian continued his journey on the *Assiniboine*.[5]

St. Louis from the River Below by George Catlin, showing Manuel Lisa's steamboat Yellowstone, on which Maximilian embarked on the trip on which he would meet Toussaint Charbonneau. (Smithsonian American Art Museum, Gift of Mrs. Joseph Harrison Jr.)

At the age of fifty-five, the prince was not an imposing figure. Alexander Culbertson, a young fur-trade clerk who accompanied him on the *Yellowstone*, drew a vivid picture: "He was a man of medium height, rather slender, sans teeth, passionately fond of his pipe, unostentatious, and speaking very broken English. His favorite dress was a white slouch hat, a black velvet coat, rather rusty from long service, and probably the greasiest pair of trousers that ever encased princely legs."[6]

Toussaint, the aging frontiersman who had lived with the Hidatsas for so long, had much to tell the visitor to the American interior. No sooner was the prince at Fort Clark than Toussaint was interpreting for him at a pipe-smoking conference with Hidatsa chiefs and warriors dressed in their best for the occasion. Later, the interpreter guided the prince to Indian ceremonies, dances and feasts.[7]

The Travellers meeting with Minatarre Indians near Fort Clark, by Karl Bodmer, showing Prince Maximilian and an interpreter believed to be Toussaint Charbonneau. (Joslyn Art Museum, Omaha, Nebraska, Gift of Enron Art Foundation)

Toussaint was helpful in other ways, intervening once when a Hidatsa warrior tried to wrest a pocket compass from around Maximilian's neck. "It was only by the assistance of old Charbonneau, that I escaped a disagreeable and, perhaps, violent scene," said the prince. This may have been the occasion on which Karl Bodmer, the twenty-three-year-old Swiss artist Maximilian had brought along to illustrate the book he planned to write, made what is believed to be the only likeness of Toussaint. The aquatint shows him with long dark hair that belied his seventy-odd years.[8]

After one day at Fort Clark, Maximilian headed on up the Missouri and stopped at the lower village of the Hidatsas. Here, Toussaint gave him "many particulars respecting these villages, in which he has lived for more than thirty years." He then said his farewells to Charbonneau and his comrades and proceeded full steam up the Missouri—to Fort Union on the *Assiniboine* and to Fort McKenzie at the mouth of the Marias River in a sixty-two-foot-long keelboat. Beyond Fort McKenzie were hostile tribes, and Maximilian was warned against going farther. A small boat was built for him and he headed downstream with a four-man crew, the artist Bodmer, two live bears, and the rest of his baggage.[9]

They had just rounded a point of land about ten miles above the Knife River on November 7 when a group of whites and Indians called to them from "some huts in a lofty wood of poplars." "We recognized old Charbonneau, and landed at once," said Maximilian. Toussaint was living with other American Fur Company employees in the hastily erected structures until better housing was built.[10]

Charbonneau piqued the prince's scientific curiosity when he mentioned there was a petrified tree trunk nearby. The next morning, Maximilian took the interpreter with him in the boat, and they landed four miles downstream to look for the tree. After crossing a frozen marsh, they found the lower part of a hollow cedar trunk, turned to stone. The trunk was too heavy to move, but the prince broke off fragments to give to an American museum.[11]

As they passed the Hidatsa villages, there was a clear sign of Toussaint's popularity among the Indians. His friends called to him to come join them. When the boat did not immediately turn toward shore, they became more vociferous. Toussaint advised Maximilian to accept the invitation. At a meeting around a warm fire in the tent of Chief Red Shield, the prince had half an hour of talk, through Toussaint, with "these friendly people." At one of the Mandan villages also, Indians came to the river bank to greet Toussaint, but he had enjoyed enough hospitality for the day, and hid himself so as not to be invited ashore again.[12]

Shortly after Maximilian's return to the fort, Toussaint invited him to a Hidatsa medicine feast. The prince, perhaps alarmed by reports that hostile Indians were near the fort, gladly accepted. Toussaint and Maximilian had to cross the Missouri to get to the Hidatsa villages, and it was tricky. The river had scarcely been frozen over for twenty-four hours.[13]

Toussaint went first, sticking poles in the ice to mark the way. Once the river was crossed, they walked for hours through the withered grass of the plain and up steep hills, through masses of prickly pear that pierced the prince's European boots. Toussaint loaned him a pair of Indian shoes, but the cactus also penetrated those.[14]

Night was falling as Toussaint, Maximilian, and Bodmer reached the Hidatsa village. Toussaint managed introductions, and then six old men advanced from a hut and stopped at the entrance of a medicine lodge. After about two hours of dancing, leaping, and singing, the women gave their undergarments to their husbands and led the elderly men to a private place in the forest. "The whole," said Maximilian, "was extremely interesting." What he did not understand was the Hidatsas' belief that the old men could transfer their skill as hunters to younger men by sleeping with their women. A day or two later, Bodmer was invited to the medicine feast again, but this time the women did not appear, and "nobody, not even Toussaint, who was so well acquainted with the Indians, could find any reason."[15]

On December 10, Toussaint took up his new quarters inside the fort. Maximilian seized the opportunity for long conversations with him about the Hidatsas. Recognizing in Toussaint a prime source of information, the prince pumped him for weather data, and Toussaint recalled a flood in which the water rose so high that only the tops of the poplars could be seen. The interpreter could not remember what year this occurred, but told the prince that such inundations were rare. Once, he remembered, the river rose rapidly at daybreak and he was forced to take high ground on top of a pile of corn, without a fire, in a cold north wind and drifting snow.[16]

Harsher duties called Toussaint away from his story telling. When the clerk of Fort Clark, a Canadian of German descent named James Kipp, received orders to make a dog sled trip to Fort Union, Toussaint went along in a horse-drawn sledge. The temperature was nineteen degrees above zero and a fierce wind was blowing when the dogs were being harnessed at eight A.M. By noon, the mercury had dropped to fourteen above. The storm drove snow through the chinks and onto the floor of the room where Maximilian was staying.[17]

By February, the snow was melting, but attacks by hostile Assiniboine Indians of the northern forests added to the hardship of the cold winter. One Assiniboine fired into a group of young people standing outside the traders' palisaded village, killing one of them. About the same time, the Assiniboines stole four horses from a hut in which Toussaint was sleeping. Hunters had trouble finding game, and food was in short supply. On February 10, the Hidatsa chief Yellow Bear rode in on horseback and presented them with a small supply of meat and a young buffalo calf. The calf seemed a "disgusting little black animal" to Maximilian but was considered "a great dainty" by the others. The grateful Toussaint put Yellow Bear up for the night in his bedroom.[18]

Maximilian came down with scurvy, but was improving by mid-April. On April 18, up and around again, he listened happily to a farewell salute from the fort's cannon and "glided rapidly down the beautiful stream of the Missouri" in the makeshift craft in which he had come.[19]

He would not see Toussaint again.

Glimpses of Baptiste

Jean Baptiste Charbonneau was something of a greenhorn when he returned to the American frontier from his sojourn in a European palace.

Quite quickly, however, he was plunged into the rigors of frontier life as a member of a group of trappers in what is now eastern Idaho. Trying an overland short-cut from the Snake River at present-day American Falls to the Wood River, they found themselves on a seventy-mile trek over lava beds crisscrossed with deep chasms that they had to leap on horseback. When they came to a chasm too broad to leap, they gave up on reaching their destination and turned to searching for water.[1]

Baptiste, suffering from heat and thirst like the rest, strayed from his companions. They feared he was dead. Spotting a campfire on a bank of the Malad River in the dead of night, he thought the campers must be hostile Indians, and Baptiste decided to retrace his steps. Meanwhile, the other trappers found the Malad and, said trapper J. H. Stevens, "drank, and laved, and drank again." Baptiste spent eleven more days of hard hiking and bitter hunger before he made it back to the Snake. When the rest of his party returned, they told him his "Indians" were a party of Hudson's Bay trappers.[2]

There were other appearances of Baptiste. Mountain man Joe Meek spotted the returned traveler near the mouth of the Platte River in 1831, clad in worn buckskin and beaded moccasins and wearing his hair shoulder length. In 1833, he was sighted at the fur trade rendezvous on the Green River in today's Wyoming, interpreting for the Shoshones and mountain man Jim Bridger. In the late 1830's, Baptiste, described as "graceful, urbane, fluent," was with Kit Carson on spring and fall buffalo hunts out of Bent's Fort, a whitewashed adobe trading post on a low bluff along the Arkansas River in present southeastern Colorado. One traveler described meeting an educated Indian in 1839 at Fort El Pueblo, five miles from Bent's Fort, and asking him, "Why did you leave civilized life for a precarious livelihood in the wilderness?" The reply, somewhat reminiscent of Baptiste's friend Duke Paul, was that he needed to "range the hills" and could not "be satisfied with the description of things, how beautiful so ever may be the style." In the spring of 1840, Baptiste was waist-deep in water as a member of a seven-man party pushing a thirty-six-foot boat, loaded with the robes and tongues of 700 buffalo, off sandbars on the notoriously shallow South Platte River. Another western traveler, W. M. Boggs, saw him working out of Bent's Fort in 1844 and 1845 and called him "the best man on foot on the plains or in the Rocky Mountains." Still another recalled Baptiste and a companion playing euchre for twenty hours straight while camped on a Bent's trading trip.[3]

John Charles Frémont came across Baptiste while heading the first of the western expeditions that would earn him the sobriquet "The Pathfinder" and make him the Republican candidate for president in 1856. The fur trade had also moved west, and

Baptiste was working as a guide for the Bent brothers—Charles, William, and George—and Ceran St. Vrain, of Bent's Fort. Frémont, catching his first glimpse of the Rocky Mountains sixty miles to the west as he made his way along the South Fork of the Platte River on a sunny July 9, 1842, spotted three men on horseback a mile or two ahead. He recognized their tall, dark-haired leader as the legendary mulatto frontiersman Jim Beckwourth. Frémont had met him earlier in his travels. Beckwourth was searching for horses that had strayed from Baptiste's island camp about eight miles upstream at Bijou's Fork, near today's Fort Morgan, Colorado. As the two men accompanying him continued the search downstream, Beckwourth guided the Frémont party to Baptiste's camp.

Baptiste had come down the river forty-five miles from Fort St. Vrain, headed for St. Louis with boats laden with profitable winter furs. He ran into low water, as was often the case on the Platte, and camped on the island, to wait for the spring flood. Baptiste christened the camp St. Helena after the island of Napoleon's exile. The forty-five Indians, French, Mexicans, Whites, and Blacks camped with him were, said one later commentator, "the plains equivalent of a lower east side neighborhood—an ethnic slumgullion stew." During a convivial evening under a grove of cottonwood trees, Baptiste sent one of his group to gather mint and, said the southerner Frémont, "concocted a very good julep." He also treated his visitors to boiled buffalo tongue and coffee with sugar, a rare treat in the wilderness. In the morning, the two explorers parted company and Frémont headed on to Bent's Fort and the Rockies.[4]

In the summer of 1843, Baptiste was at Fort Laramie in today's Wyoming with another mixed company, this one organized by the Scottish adventurer Sir William Drummond Stewart. The veteran mountain man William Sublette described the group as made up of forty-five "doctors, Lawyers, Botanists, Bugg Ketchers, Hunters and men of nearly all professions." One was even an actor. Baptiste was employed as a driver of one of the party's twenty red-painted mule-drawn supply carts, and frequently grumbled about the mules' recalcitrance. Once, he doubled as the whip-wielding referee of a fist fight that ended in gunfire. He also took part in a foray into the mountains to capture bighorn and prong-horn sheep alive. Some of the animals ended up on Drummond's estate in Scotland, but Baptiste stayed on in the American West that his father had penetrated nearly four decades before.[5]

"Doctors, Lawyers, Botanists, Bugg Ketchers, Hunters and men of nearly all professions." *Our Camp* by Alfred Jacob Miller shows the William Drummond Stewart party that mountain man William Sublette described. (Buffalo Bill Historical Center, Cody, Woming; Gift of the Coe Foundation; 11.70)

Desolation on the Missouri

Francis Chardon kept a daily count of the rats killed at Fort Clark. But he had given up counting deaths among the Indians—"they die so fast that it is impossible."[1]

The year 1837 was the worst in the three frustrating years during which Chardon, a Philadelphian of French extraction who traded on the Upper Missouri for twenty years, had been in charge of the fortified American Fur Company trading post.[2]

Smallpox was raging among the Mandans and Hidatsas. The Indians blamed the traders for bringing the infection. Game was scarce, and hunger threatened everywhere. No wonder Toussaint Charbonneau, now at Fort Clark as interpreter, was welcome whenever he arrived from a trip to the Mandan villages with fresh meat.[3]

Only two weeks before, a young Mandan had come to the whitewashed fort with a cocked gun under his robe and tried to kill Chardon. One of the trader's men grabbed the intruder and turned him over to the Indians before he could fire, but the incident put Chardon on his guard.[4]

Now word came that the Hidatsas were "bent on the destruction of us all." The seasoned frontiersman suspected the report was false, but wanted to make sure. So he sent Toussaint to the Indian villages with a supply of tobacco and "a bag full of good talk." His interpreter, he said, would bring the straight news.

Toussaint relayed word that the Hidatsas had no thought of attacking the traders, but that their enemies, the Arikaras, had been making threats. "Which of the two, to believe, I Know not," Chardon recorded, "however, I will still be on my guard."[5]

The episode shed further light on the important role played by Toussaint during the warfare, disease, and famine that plagued the Missouri River fur trade in its most terrible decade. By this time, he had been among the tribes of the upper Missouri for more than forty years. For more than thirty years, he had worked among American explorers and fur traders. He was hired as an interpreter on July 1, 1835, by W. N. Fulkerson, the Mandan sub agent for the Indian Affairs bureau. Over and over, Toussaint was the one to turn to for valuable information.[6]

Chardon cannot have been easy to work for in the best of times. Prince Maximilian, visiting him at his previous post at Fort Union, found him cheerful and courteous, but others painted a different picture. Among a hard-drinking lot of men, he was noted for being excessively fond of whiskey, once finishing off most of a guest's two-gallon jug with swigs at fifteen-minute intervals. One of his succession of Indian wives was given "a good whipping" for failing to mend his moccasins.[7]

There was plenty at Fort Clark to exacerbate his temper. Buffalo, valued for the table as well as the fur market, were scarce. As for rats, there were plenty. In March of 1835 alone, 110 were killed, in April, 130. As spring broke in 1836, Chardon reflected that of many winters in Indian country he had "never spent a more unpleasant one."[8]

Into this atmosphere, Toussaint brought his gift of gab, his woodsman's craftiness, and, not least, his culinary skills. One of the first times Chardon mentioned him in his journal, it was for giving "a feast to the Indians." For the first Christmas at the fort, the interpreter prepared a supper of meat pies, bread, fricasseed pheasants, boiled tongue, roast beef and coffee. For the Feast of the Epiphany, a January 6 Christian festival more observed by the French than the Americans, he prepared pudding pies and fried and roasted meat. At another meal, Chardon declared his mince pie "charming."[9]

At the age of almost seventy-six, Toussaint's adventures among Native American women continued unabated. In the fall of 1834, Chardon recorded that the interpreter had two lovely Indian wives. One of them ran away, back to the Hidatsa village she came from. On October 22, 1834, Toussaint left the fort in quest of her, with his other wife in tow. "Poor Old Man," said Chardon.[10]

Toussaint apparently did not get his missing wife back, but he returned from the Indian settlement "with all sorts of talk. " The aging interpreter remained a font of information. Chardon thought it was too much sometimes. On April 30, 1835, he said, Toussaint arrived "with an over stock of Indian News—from all quarters." Most of it was bad. There was fear of attacks from the Sioux.[11]

Plentiful though the news might be, the traders were not getting what they came for. At the height of the 1835-36 season, Toussaint returned from a trip to the villages in bitterly cold weather with thirty buffalo robes—a poor haul for two months of trading. The great days of the fur trade were beginning what would be a long decline.[12]

On January 11, 1836, as a Hidatsa boy was visiting in the interpreter's room at the fort, two bullets whizzed through Toussaint's hat. Neither he nor his visitor was hurt but it was, said Chardon, a narrow escape from a "daring attempt at revenge." A band of Yankton Sioux, driven by hunger from their usual hunting grounds to camps near the villages, had been attacked that day by Hidatsas as they marched up the Knife River. An estimated

150 were killed and forty-three women and children taken prisoner. Of eight or ten who escaped and rushed to the fort with the news, one had lost all his family in the attack. It was he who fired at the Hidatsa boy.[13]

For a month, Toussaint had been ill with "something like the Cholic." When summer arrived, he decided to leave his quarters in the fort and live at his home village of Metaharta, keeping Chardon advised from there. By the next December, he was back at the fort. The Mandans and Hidatsas were starving and the fort was full of men, women, and children begging meat. Even the horses were exhausted, refusing to pull fuel carts up the hill on which the trading post was perched. "I do not Know what we shall do for fire wood," wrote Chardon.[14]

In March, 1837, a figure more flamboyant than any Toussaint had ever known arrived at Fort Clark. His name was James Dickson, but he had persuaded a band of would-be adventurers, some of them recruited from the fur trade, that he was Montezuma II, destined to liberate the Indians of New Mexico and California. Handsome, bearded, and a good talker who liked to quote poetry, he had arrived in Washington from somewhere in the winter of 1835-1836, saying he was raising recruits for the independence of Texas.[15]

As he made his way westward, his objectives changed. He proclaimed himself a general and gathered an "army" of about sixty men to help him conquer Mexico. He said he had talked with Indian chiefs while in Washington, and they had promised him a fighting force of two to three thousand. By the time he reached Lake Huron, his "army" had dwindled to twelve.[16]

When he reached Fort Clark, virtually alone, he was still putting up a brave front. "I was Presented today with a Sword, from Mr. Dickson—the Liberator of all Indians," Chardon noted on March 21. He did not say whether Dickson still had with him the suit of mail in which he had sometimes chosen to strut. Four days later, the liberator and one of the fort's hired hands headed for Fort Union in two canoes.[17]

On June 14, Toussaint reported that he had met him a few miles above the fort. The canoeists had found the going hard, and Dickson had turned back on foot. He was, said Toussaint, "tired of walking, and has laid himself down to die." Dickson was never heard from again. The comic opera had come to a tragic ending. [18]

The misadventures of the preposterous Montezuma II gave way to high drama on June 19, 1837, when the American Fur Company steamboat *St. Peter's* chugged around a bend below Fort Clark. "All hands a Frolicking," wrote Chardon next day, when the cargo was unloaded. The *St. Peter's* was making its annual run with goods to be traded to the Indians for furs. But the vessel also had something else aboard: smallpox. The disease had been breaking out periodically among the Mandans and Hidatsas for more than half a century, but now it was to smite them as never before.[19]

As the steamboat paddled its way toward its next stop at Fort Union, all seemed serene at Fort Clark. Toussaint cooked a celebratory dinner for the Fourth of July, and Chardon drank a toast to one of his heroes, Andrew Jackson. Ten days later, the first Mandan died of smallpox. Several others caught it. The threat of disease was added to the danger of starvation facing the thirty men at the fort.[20]

In addition to condemning the traders for bringing the plague upon them, the tribes quarreled among themselves. "We are beset by enemies on all sides—expecting to be shot every Minute," wrote Chardon. The Mandan warrior Four Bears said as he lay dying, "I have Never Called a White Man a Dog, but today, I do Pronounce them to be a set of Black Harted Dogs."[21]

Jacob Halsey, who had captained the *St. Peter's* on its fateful trip, told his superiors in St. Louis that only four died out of twenty-seven who contracted the disease. Perhaps he was only trying to protect himself from blame; elsewhere, he estimated that ten out of every twelve persons afflicted died. Death came within a few agonizing hours—the victim suffering pains in the back and head. The bodies, turned black and hideously swollen, were tossed into the bushes or dumped over the cliff on which Fort Clark stood.[22]

New cases were reported every day. On August 11, the remaining Mandans abandoned their village and moved across the Missouri. Two days later, the disease broke out inside the walls of the fort. On August 19, Chardon reported that "Charbonneau and his family" had left the previous night for Metaharta. So dangerous did the traders find the atmosphere that Toussaint crept out of the fort under cover of darkness rather than risk riding through the countryside by daylight. He returned alone on September 10. His wife had died of smallpox four days before.[23]

The ravages of smallpox were not the only change in the landscape in which Toussaint had lived and worked for so long. As early as 1831, trader William Gordon reported gloomily to Clark, "The diminution of furs in the upper Missouri and in the Rocky Mountains is general and extensive, and has been very great since my first adventures to these countries ten years ago." No longer, Gordon said, was it worth the expense to send an expedition exclusively in search of the once-rich fur trade.[24]

Through it all, Toussaint went about his work as best he could. Five days after his wife's death, again traveling by night, he took two mule loads of powder, ball, and tobacco to the Hidatsa villages and traded them for eighty-four buffalo robes and four beaver skins. Two days later, he was off again with a small amount of goods with which to trade during the winter. In October, with so many Indians dead and others decamped from the area, the danger of massacre had abated. On December 31, Toussaint returned from his Hidatsa village to report that only ten lodges remained. The rest had moved to the Little Missouri River. He had heard nothing from them.[25]

The year 1838 opened with foul weather and the smallpox still raging. Horses and mules died in bitter winds from the northwest. Thousands of buffalo, seeking shelter from the storms, could be seen from the fort. But it was too cold to hunt buffalo, or even to go out and cut fire wood. Toussaint was making more frequent trading forays, but trade was slow. In February, Chardon reported that "My Old Cook and his Indian family had a dispute." This may have been Toussaint.[26]

Charles Larpenteur and a companion, paddling their canoe downstream about seventy miles west of Fort Clark in late March, nervously eyed a group of hostile-looking Indians on the south bank. Their fears were allayed when they spotted Toussaint, in pants and a red flannel shirt, amid the Indians. Toussaint advised the traders which Indians to make gifts of tobacco to, and they paddled on, happy to find themselves "befriended instead of butchered."[27]

As he did on the Lewis and Clark expedition, Toussaint ran into trouble on the water. As he paddled toward the fort in a strong cold northwest wind on the night of April 11, a sudden gust caught his skin canoe and dumped its load of 600 buffalo robes into the Missouri. Chardon sent two men to help him. Struggling with strong winds, they hauled the canoe out of the water, recovered the robes and tried to dry them. On the 19th, Toussaint beached his canoe at the fort with 400 robes, still wet. The hides were distributed to Indian women to dress, each woman receiving a fifth of those she processed.[28]

Indians were still dying of smallpox. In February, Joshua Pilcher, the former merchant-banker and fur trader who was now government agent to the Sioux, had offered to escort a federal health officer upriver in the spring to vaccinate the Indians. Clark placed Pilcher in temporary charge of the Mandan sub-agency. Early in April, he visited Indian villages along the Missouri in the American Fur Company steamboat *Antelope*, accompanied by a physician who inoculated an estimated 3,000 Indians.[29]

Some people thought the vaccinations came none too soon. Jefferson had instructed Meriwether Lewis to "Carry with you some matter of the kine pox; inform those of them with whom you may be, of it's efficacy as a preservative from the smallpox; & instruct & encourage them in the use of it." By the time he reached Cincinnati, however, Lewis had experimented with the vaccine and found it no longer effective, so it apparently was not taken among the tribes he visited later.[30]

At any rate, Jefferson's farsighted view on Indian inoculations did not take hold in all Washington councils. Although Congress voted funds for the vaccination of Indians as early as 1832, Secretary of War Lewis Cass promptly decreed that "no effort would be made . . . under any circumstances . . . to send a surgeon higher up the Missouri than the Mandans, and I think not higher than the Aricaras." This could have denied vaccine to the tribes most in need of it.[31]

Pilcher calculated the smallpox killed 17,000 Indians. This was almost certainly an exaggeration. Other calculations set the figure at 15,000, or less. The most precise tally of survivors among the Mandans was twenty-three men, forty women, and sixty or seventy youngsters. The Jesuit missionary Father Pierre-Jean De Smet, passing through the area two years later, was told that "only seven families escaped the contagion" and that eighty warriors committed suicide. More than ninety per cent of the once-powerful Mandan tribe was wiped out.[32]

On the snowy Saturday night of October 27, 1838, with the epidemic at last over, Toussaint bedded yet another bride. His choice this time was a fourteen-year-old Assiniboine girl captured by the Arikaras in a battle that summer and, said Chardon, "bought by me." The young men of the fort and two Arikaras gave Toussaint a traditional charivari, beating on drums, pans, and kettles and firing off guns in a raucous celebration of his wedding night. Two Indians, who had never seen or heard such a festivity

Fort Clark on the Missouri by Karl Bodmer. Here Toussaint Charbonneau lived through the smallpox and starvation that scourged the upper Missouri in the years 1835-38. "God send better times for the future," wrote Chardon. (Joslyn Art Museum, Omaha, Nebraska)

before, scuttled away for fear they would be killed. Toussaint showed his appreciation to the men of the fort by fixing them a feast and treating them to a glass of grog. Then, said Chardon, he "went to bed with his young wife, with the intention of doing his best."[33]

The ranks of the Indians Toussaint lived with were thinned. The fur-bearing animals that had been his livelihood were dwindling. But as in his errand-running days on the Assiniboine River, in the boats with Lewis and Clark, bargaining for furs with Manuel Lisa or struggling with the smallpox at Fort Clark, he had the intention of doing his best. Touissaint Charbonneau's zest for life, which had led him to accept the challenge of a transcontinental journey in middle age, was undimmed as he approached the "last scene of all, that ends this strange, eventful history."[34]

One year later, he made his pilgrimage to St. Louis to collect his final pay.

Now Jean Baptiste would take the stage.

CHAPTER THIRTEEN

Westward Once More

On May 13, 1846, a Congress caught up in the fever for west-ward expansion declared war on Mexico, and Baptiste Charbonneau found himself enlisted in a mission that was to change his life. As an adult as he had been as a child, he was to be in the vanguard of one of the great westward movements of nine-teenth century America. Baptiste signed on as a guide to General Stephen W. Kearny on an expedition to occupy New Mexico and California, and Kearny assigned him to the Mormon Battalion.[1]

Members of the rapidly growing Latter-Day Saints (Mormon) church had not much wanted to join the U.S. Army. As they saw it, the army had failed to protect them from persecution and mob action that had driven them from Illinois and Missouri to Iowa. Their leaders, however, had a different view. One, former Post-master General Amos Kendall, urged President James Knox Polk to "assist our emigration by enlisting one thousand of our men, arming, equipping and establishing them in California to defend the country."[2]

At the White House, other advantages were seen. Polk's cabinet ordered Kearny to enlist a few hundred Saints "to conciliate them, attach them to our country, and prevent them from taking part against us." At the urging of Brigham Young and other leaders, reluctant Mormons agreed to enlist, and a battalion of about 500 was formed. All but six soldiers, their commander and a few regular army officers were members of the church.[3]

Lieutenant Colonel Philip St. George Cooke, the Virginia-born son of a Revolutionary War surgeon and a veteran of frontier Army posts, was named to command the battalion. Cooke reached Santa Fe on October 7, assumed command and received orders from Kearny to "open a wagon road to the Pacific."[4]

Kearny had gone on west ahead of him, taking Baptiste and the other guides. A few days out of Santa Fe, Colonel W. H. Emery spotted what he thought were cedar trees, so far away that they looked like shrubs. Baptiste knew better. "Indians! They are Apache," he called out. Emery acknowledged that the guide's "more practical eye" detected human figures in what he thought was shrubbery.[5]

Kearny told Cooke he would have his guides reconnoiter and return to Santa Fe to advise him on the best route to follow. He seemed also to have a pretty firm idea what route this would be—the one he had chosen, following the Rio Grande to somewhere near present-day Truth or Consequences, New Mexico, and then cutting west overland to the Gila River.[6]

When Baptiste, dispatched by Kearny, joined the battalion near Albuquerque on October 24, he told Cooke that he and the other guides disagreed with the general. They favored a longer route that would take them south of the present Mexican border and then to the San Pedro River and downstream to its confluence with the Gila southeast of today's Phoenix, Arizona. Cooke was skeptical. "They did not make a thorough examination by any means , and the practicability of the route . . . is still a problem."

His doubts aside, the members of the battalion knew their mission was clear: they must get to the Pacific.[7]

Their commander, a full-bearded man with a stern gaze and a beak-like nose, was a strict disciplinarian who sprinkled his commands with "a rare combination of swear words." But he gave Baptiste his due. No less than twenty-nine times, Cooke mentioned his services in his journal—selecting routes, trapping beaver, finding water, establishing camps, discovering passes, scouting and, more successfully than his father, hunting grizzlies. He may also have been conversant with Indian sign language. Captain Henry S. Turner, acting adjutant-general of the Army of the West, informing Cooke that an Apache chief had promised to send "some of his young men to conduct you to a good route," added that the Apaches would not know Spanish but "it is probable that Charboneaux will understand [and] make himself understood by them by signs."[8]

As they began their trek though rough, broken country dotted here and there with ancient ruins, Baptiste and the other guides "were fearful and quite downcast" at rumors that Mexicans in the area might attack them. Cooke, seeking to dispel their fears, "maintained an air of indifference," Sergeant Daniel Tyler would recall.[9]

On November 8, the guides returned from exploring the land ahead and said they thought it would be impossible to get through with wagons.[10]

With his recruits facing 300 miles through land unknown to them, Cooke wrote, "It has now become obvious to all that we cannot go on so with any prospect of a successful or safe termination to the expedition." With twenty-two men on the sick list and rations running short, the commander sent fifty-five of the sick and least efficient men back to Santa Fe. "Solemn times for us," wrote Private Henry Standage. "May the God of Heaven protect us all."[11]

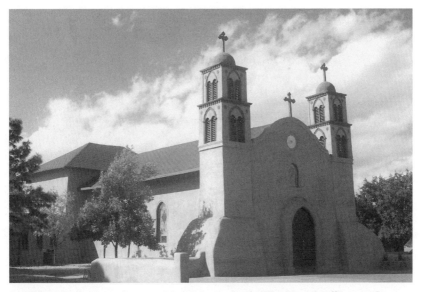

San Miguel Mission in Socorro, New Mexico, built 1819-21 and still in use. Socorro was the first sizable settlement the battalion met after leaving Santa Fe. As they approached it, Col. W. H. Emery noted, "The church, as usual . . . meets the eye at a great distance." (Photo by Joyce Miller Nelson)

Four days later, the battalion left the Rio Grande about fifteen miles northwest of present Rincon, New Mexico. The colonel sent Baptiste, his fellow guide Antoine Leroux, and five other men forward two days later. They were instructed to make "an active and more distant examination of the country" and send a man back daily to report. The two literate and knowledgeable guides should have been good company for each other. Leroux later became a wealthy and prominent citizen who served as a delegate at the New Mexico Territorial Organization Convention.[12]

The next day Baptiste was back, reporting that a gap in the mountains was passable, there was water six miles ahead, and the plains beyond were "very pretty." The six miles to water turned out to be three. Beyond that point, Cooke encountered new species of cactus and partridges, "But, alas, where shall the water be found?" On November 18, they crossed the Mimbres River in what

Mormon Battalion Monument five miles northeast of San Felipe Pueblo, New Mexico. The monument, erected in 1940, is near the dead end of a road reached via exit 257 on Interstate 25. The battalion crossed the site on October 21, 1846, on their way from the Galisteo River to the Rio Grande Valley. (Photo by Joyce Miller Nelson)

is now southwestern New Mexico. "The brethren are daily growing weak," wrote Standage.[13]

The rest of the guides found one water hole, but in the ten or twelve miles beyond that there was no water. The colonel held a crucial meeting with all of the guides after taking them up a hill 300 or 400 feet high to look over the country near the present New Mexico-Arizona border. Should he continue the circuit to the south favored by Baptiste and the others? The maps he had were worthless, Cooke complained. "I have reflected long and anxiously. What difference if this distance is doubled, if it is a better route? I shall strike the Gila all the same by either." It would be the southern route.[14]

Still, he was worried, and "much dissatisfied" with the course Baptiste had chosen. On November 22, he "feared for tomorrow night." His fears eased the next day when he saw white smoke, a signal from Leroux that he had found a water hole. During a hard day of searching, Baptiste located a trail to Leroux's location. Coming back after dark, he gave his exhausted mule a half-hour rest and feed stop, then tried to mount it. The mule kicked him and ran off. Unable to catch the animal, he shot it to keep his saddle and pistols from falling into the hands of the Apaches.[15]

They reached the water hole the next day, after forty miles without a drop to drink, but the men had to remain thirsty a while longer. They lapped at the water, captured it with spoons or sucked it through quills, but could not get enough to slake their thirst.[16]

Baptiste, crossing the mountains in search of the best way ahead, found smooth going, "as easy as a railroad," on a dry lake bed with a surface that looked like ice. He had encountered what is now Playas Lake—still dry most of the time—in Hidalgo County, New Mexico.[17]

On November 25—a cold, windless day, probably ten to fifteen degrees above zero—the battalion neared Guadalupe Canyon, straddling the border between present New Mexico and Arizona.

Here Baptiste, like Toussaint Charbonneau before him, encountered the grizzly bear. Cooke saw him approach a mother and her two cubs "standing conspicuously and looking quite white in the sun." Baptiste felled the adult bear with his second shot, and escaped the fiercely crying cubs by climbing onto a rock. Cooke's gaze was drawn by the red shirt that Baptiste, like his father, sometimes wore. The commander had hired a Mexican guide to help them through the mountains, and the linguist Baptiste cried out in Spanish to him for more ammunition. The cubs escaped.[18]

Cooke still thought they could have found a better route. "My guides are ignorant of the country," he grumbled. By December 9, the guides had become doubtful themselves. But the battalion pushed on. Finally, just twenty paces away, they saw "a fine, bold stream." They had reached the San Pedro.[19]

Three days later, Baptiste spotted a gap through the mountains to the west that he believed to be "the one that we are to pass." He recommended they leave the San Pedro and take a cutoff to the Gila. The shortcut would save valuable time, but in its path was a Mexican garrison at Tucson, one-hundred soldiers with two brass cannon. The next morning, at camp on the San Pedro, Cooke issued Order Number 19 from Mormon Battalion headquarters. "Thus far on our course to California," the order said, "we have followed the guides furnished by the general. These guides now point to Tucson . . . We will march then to Tucson. We came not to make war against Sonora, and less still to destroy an unimportant outpost of defense against Indians. But we will take the straight course before us and overcome all resistance."[20]

There was no resistance. As Cooke implied, northern Sonora was by 1846 largely under Apache control. The commander of the garrison at Tucson chose to evacuate the town and send twenty-five men to the Gila to harass Cooke's party along its route. After reaching the cottonwoods of the Gila near the future site of Florence, Arizona, four days before Christmas, the commander sent out Leroux, Baptiste and three other guides with instructions to proceed with caution if they saw any sign of Mexican troops. They met none.[21]

Cooke was beginning to think his guides had steered him right after all. "Will not this prove the best emigrant's road from Independence to California, by the route I came?" he asked. It was a good question. The Saints and their commander, with the aid of Jean Baptiste Charbonneau, had in fact opened a wagon route that was used by thousands of emigrants and followed along parts of its way by the Atchison, Topeka & Santa Fe and Southern Pacific railroads.[22]

The battalion's task was not easy. At one point, water was so scarce that sentinels were posted to keep the men from dipping it with their canteens. Men marched with their feet wrapped in woolen or cotton cloth. Mules fell and were drowned as they crossed the Colorado River. "At best, our prospect is bad," the colonel declared. On a pole above what looked like a dry well, he read a note from Baptiste: "No water, January 2nd, Charbonneau." Cooke wrote, "This fills me with fearfulness for success and safety,"[23]

By mid-January, they had arrived in today's Imperial County, California. Baptiste went ahead to reconnoiter and rejoined the battalion near what is now the San Diego County line. It was at least a hard five days march to their destination, he said, and supplies there were meager. Mexican forces were concentrated in a pueblo. It was under attack from the north by Fremont, who was in trouble with Mexican authorities for taking too close a look at their coastal settlements while supposedly seeking a better road for emigrants to Oregon. From the south, the pueblo was menaced by Kearny. Cooke would approach from the east, hemming the enemy in. On January 23 came word that the hot-headed Frémont had occupied the pueblo. The battalion changed course and marched straight for San Diego.[24]

On their way they passed the deserted Catholic mission of San Luis Rey, described by Cooke as "a fine large church of stuccoed brick, with an immense quadrangle of apartments with a corridor, and pillars and arches on each side within and on one face without." There were wine cellars, and paintings on the walls. The French trading ship master August Duhaut-Cilly, visiting the mission in 1827, found the wine "the best . . . in all California" and took some of it home with him. Around a sundial in the center of the court were orange, pepper, fig, and olive trees, as well as ornamental plants. A bell hung silent in the steeple.[25]

A U.S. Boundary Commission inspector who visited the mission a few years later described it as a place where "a prince or a nabob might luxuriate to his heart's content."[26]

There were no princes or nabobs in the weary battalion. But particularly to Baptiste, a Catholic in an army of Mormons, the mission must have seemed like heaven after the long march.

Veduta della Missione di San Luis-Rey nella California

Painting of Mission San Luis Rey, by Auguste Duhaut-Cilly. A place where "a prince or a nabob might luxuriate to his heart's content." (California Historical Society; FN-04585)

Three miles further on, the men ascended a bluff from which "the long, long looked for great Pacific Ocean appeared plain to our view." Like his father at Cape Disappointment, Baptiste doubtless joined Sergeant Tyler in feeling "the joy, the cheer that filled our souls."[27]

A week later, they marched into San Diego by moonlight and Cooke rode down to report to his general. In the first order issued from his new headquarters, the colonel told the battalion: "History may be searched in vain for an equal march of infantry."[28]

Baptiste was in San Diego on April 16, when Lydia Hunter, the wife of his friend Captain Jesse D. Hunter, one of the battalion's Mormon officers, gave birth to a son in their quarters there. She had been pregnant ever since the battalion left Ft. Leavenworth. They named the boy Diego. Six days later, Lydia Hunter died. A fellow officer wrote in his journal, "The guide, Charbonneau, was very kind and helpful to Captain Hunter during this sad time."[29]

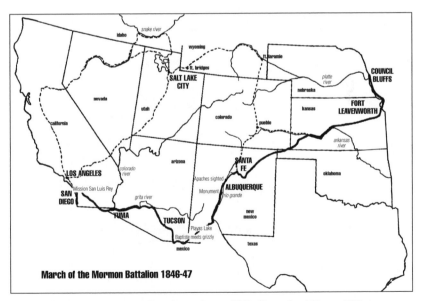

March of the Mormon Battalion 1846-47

Route of the Mormon Battalion from Council Bluffs to San Diego. "History may be searched in vain for an equal march of infantry." (Used by permission, Utah State Historical Society, all rights reserved)

The march of the Mormon battalion had brought Baptiste Charbonneau to the Pacific, just as the epic exploration of Lewis and Clark had brought his father. But there would be no trip back for Baptiste. The West would remain his home.

John B. Charbonneau

Baptiste had not seen the last of Mission San Luis Rey.

General Kearny was mistaken when he believed he was being sent ahead to California to assume command of a defeated enemy. The Mexicans still held everything between San Diego and Santa Barbara, and his men would have to fight every inch of the way. The Mormon Battalion was sent back to the deserted mission with orders to clean it up, garrison it as a military post and hold it against the enemy if need be. In July, 1847, when U.S. forces finally took California, the mission was made headquarters of the Indian sub-agency for the southern military district, with Baptiste's friend Captain Hunter in charge. The battalion's commanders also recognized Baptiste's ability to be more than a guide. On November 24, acting military governor Richard B. Mason sent Colonel J. D. Stevenson, commander of the district, a blank appointment for "alcalde," or justice of the peace, of the sub-agency, leaving a blank to be filled in with Baptiste's name or any other name. Baptiste got the job, most likely on the recommendation of Hunter.[1]

It seemed like pleasant duty. The cleaned-up mission, complete with two large vineyards and a reservoir for bathing and washing, lay in a fertile valley near the present city of Oceanside, about fifty miles north of San Diego. But problems came with Baptiste's job. Under the orders of Colonel Mason, as relayed by Lieutenant William Tecumseh Sherman, (later to become famous for his merciless march through Georgia as a Union general in the Civil War) Baptiste was to help Hunter take protective charge of the Indians living at the mission, "draw them gradually to habits of order" and prevent them from "leading an idle, thriftless life." The Indians were paid twelve and one-half cents per day, presumably in addition to their board. The payment was seldom in cash, but generally in goods from a store and liquor shop three doors away from the mission church. If they ran up a bill exceeding the amount they had coming for their work, they would be required to work it off. Records showed that by far the greater part of purchases at the store was for brandy, whiskey or wine. Essentially, the laborers were being paid in liquor.[2]

It was part of Baptiste's day's work on April 24, 1848, to sentence a Luiseno Indian named Fulgencio to work off a debt of $51.37 and one-half cent to liquor store proprietor Jose Antonio Pico at the rate of his twelve and one-half cent daily wages. Such treatment made the Indians restive, and Baptiste was accused of being involved in a planned insurrection. He denied the charge in a statement that he gave under the name "John B. Charbonneau of St. Louis." In letters written in Spanish and English as alcalde, he was signing himself "J. B. Charbonneau." He resigned after less than a year, saying his Indian blood made it impossible for him to be impartial. Colonel Stevenson said that Baptiste had served diligently but "being a half-breed Indian of the U.S. is regarded by the people as favoring Indians more than he should do, and hence there is much complaint against him."[3]

Hunter also offered to resign, but was given a six months' leave of absence instead, beginning December 17, 1848. His leave came in hectic times. Eleven months earlier, a carpenter named James W. Marshall had found gold nuggets in a mill race on the American River in northern California, setting off the gold rush of 1849. Baptiste, very likely accompanied by Hunter, joined it and was reunited with his old companion Jim Beckwourth. The fabled mountain man had set out across country from Stockton in the unlikely role of clothing salesman and set up shop in Sonora, a thriving tent city of nearly 2,000 in the midst of the richest diggings. [4]

Riding into Murderer's Bar on the American River's North Fork, Beckwourth found his old friend Baptiste keeping house there and moved in with him until the rainy season came. In addition to going partners in a mining venture, the pair may have run the house as a sort of hotel. Traveler James Haley White, who claimed to have gone to school with Baptiste in St. Louis, referred to it as a hotel in saying he stayed there on his way from Sacramento to the gold fields in 1849.[5]

While Baptiste panned for gold, his old benefactor Duke Paul, making his last visit to America, called on Colonel John Sutter, at whose mill Marshall had found the nuggets that touched off the gold rush. The duke could not help noticing that a Shoshone youth employed by Sutter bore a "startling likeness" to the young man he had befriended on the Missouri sixteen years before.[6]

By 1852, Baptiste was settled in the Auburn, California area, the hub of five wagon roads fanning out into rich gold country. The 1860 census listed John B. Charbonneau, fifty-seven years old, as living at Secret Ravine, about ten miles from Auburn. A city directory a year later showed him working as a desk clerk at Auburn's Orleans Hotel, a brick hostelry on the town's Main Street that advertised itself as "one of the best public houses in the country," taking "Boarders . . . by the Day or Week at the lowest rates."[7]

But hotel-clerking was not the life for the son of Toussaint Charbonneau and Sacagawea. He pricked up his ears at news of yet another gold strike.

Gold had been discovered in Montana as early as 1852, but for a decade attracted little attention. Then, on July 28, 1862, three prospectors just off a wagon train from Denver City went panning in a stream they called Grasshopper Creek, the same stream Lewis and Clark had named Willard's Creek in honor of sturdy Private Alexander Willard. By whatever name, the creek was a bonanza for John White, Charles Reville, and William Still. [8]

They were not the only ones. On May 26, 1863, gold was struck on a then-unnamed creek near Virginia City, and the rush to Alder Gulch was on. In six years, the district yielded ten million dollars worth of gold. Gold-seekers headed west over wagon tracks now so heavily traveled that there were guide books for them. Others came from the by-now-exhausted diggings of California, and Baptiste and two partners, one of them probably Captain Hunter, joined the trek in the spring of 1866. [9]

Baptiste probably did not know it, but his mother's people were in desperate straits in the country he was headed for. The once-proud Lemhi Shoshone were described by Indian agent Major John Owens in 1861 as "poor miserable, naked starving wretches" whose situation "language is inadequate to describe." Weirs built by white settlers along the Lemhi River prevented salmon from swimming upstream to spawn—thus depriving the Lemhi of their chief source of food. They migrated some one hundred miles east and set up lodges near Virginia City, where, said Owens, they were "robd Murdered their women outraged etc." by unprincipled gold-seekers. More powerful neighboring tribes robbed them of their horses. No longer could they travel to the Three Forks country to hunt buffalo, as they had in the days of Lewis and Clark. How Baptiste might have responded to the plight of Sacagawea's tribe will never be known. Before departing, he stopped at the Auburn Placer-Herald office and "said he was going to leave California, probably for good, as he was about returning to familiar scenes." He was sixty-one years old and, the editor said, felt he had "few remaining days . . . in store for him."[10]

He spoke more truly than he knew. Fording the icy Owyhee River in southeastern Oregon, Baptiste took a chill. His companions helped him to a fortified hostel and general store, Inskip Station, on a toll road twenty-five miles to the northeast, where he died of pneumonia on May 16. Before heading on to Montana, his comrades sent word of his death to a friend in Auburn, who passed it on to the *Placer-Herald*. They also gave the news to the *Owyhee Avalanche* in Ruby City, a few miles across the Oregon border into Idaho. On June 2, the Idaho paper carried a brief obituary, misstating Baptiste's name as I. B. Charbonneau, adding two years to his age, and giving his birthplace as St. Louis instead of

Ruins of Inskip Station near Danner, Oregon, where Baptiste died after fording the Owyhee River en route to the Montana gold fields. Leaving Auburn, he felt he had "few remaining days . . . in store for him." (Photo by Joyce Miller Nelson)

Lewis and Clark's palisade at the Mandan Villages. The editor said he had "received a note (don't know who from) dated May 16" requesting the publication.[11]

In Auburn, the newspaper of his latter-day home town recalled him as "a good meaning and inoffensive man" who had made himself "known to most of the pioneer citizens of this region" in his fourteen years there. The eulogy appeared on the editorial page, after an item announcing a new four-horse stage line between Auburn and El Dorado County. [12]

Baptiste is buried near Danner, Oregon, in a windswept area still so sparsely populated a century and a third later that the mail is delivered only three days a week. He lies in a grave marked with a historical placard, surrounded by sagebrush, rimmed by distant mountains, about 250 miles southwest of his mother's birthplace.

Burial place of Baptiste Charbonneau, "a good meaning and inoffensive man," with a historical marker placed by state of Oregon near Danner, Oregon. (Photo by Joyce Miller Nelson)

Epilogue

In 1907, the *Journal of American History* published an article by Grace Raymond Hebard, a librarian and professor at the University of Wyoming, entitled, "Woman Who Led the Way to the Golden West: Pilot of the First White Men to Cross America."

We must take a look at this article, and writings that echoed it, because many people believe them, and if they are true, then much of what has been said in this book is false.

To Hebard, the woman who died at Fort Manuel in 1812 was not Sacagawea but another Shoshone wife of Toussaint Charbonneau. She identified this other wife as Otter Woman.

The real Sacagawea, she said, lived to a great age, spent time with the Comanches in Oklahoma, and died on the Wind River Reservation in Wyoming on April 9, 1884.[1]

On that morning, a woman sometimes known as Porivo was found dead in her tepee by her apparently adopted son Bazil, with whom she lived. The Rev. John Roberts, the Episcopal missionary who presided at her funeral, entered her name in the Parish Register of Burials as "Bazil's Mother." Roberts said he knew little about the Lewis and Clark expedition at the time, but later learned that the woman was Sacagawea.[2]

A year before his mother's death, Roberts reported, Bazil told him that he didn't know her exact age but she must have been about one hundred years old. Accordingly, the cleric entered her age as one hundred. This would mean she was born in 1784 and would have been sixteen or seventeen when Sacagawea was captured by the Hidatsas. Lewis said in his journal that at that time Sacagawea had not reached the age of puberty, which he said the Indians reckoned at thirteen or fourteen. Curiously, Hebard said in her article that Sacagawea was five years old when captured, which would have made her only ten when Baptiste was born.[3]

Grace Raymond Hebard of the University of Wyoming wrote that Sacagawea lived a long life and died on the Wind River Reservation in Wyoming. She stuck to her opinion despite "ridicule, doubt, suspicion, denial" by other historians. (Photo Courtesy American Heritage Center, University of Wyoming)

Grace Hebard was a highly respected person in Wyoming, and remained so nearly a century later. A research room in the University of Wyoming's American Heritage Center bears her name and contains her voluminous and detailed research files. In a forty-five-year career with the university, she served as librarian, trustee, and professor of political economy and western history. At her death in 1936, she was eulogized as the state's "most eminent historian" and a leader in the struggle for women's rights.[4]

Nevertheless, her theory of Sacagawea's life and death was greeted with, in her own words, "ridicule, doubt, suspicion, denial" as other historians found flaws of fact and reasoning. In 1924, the Commissioner of Indian Affairs asked Charles Eastman, a physician, author and lecturer who was a Sioux Indian, to look into the controversy. Eastman reported that the woman buried on the Wind River Reservation was indeed Sacagawea.[5]

This did not end the matter. Much of Eastman's report was based on hearsay, sometimes at second or third hand. He quoted, for instance, information provided by an eighty-year-old woman who had heard it from her father when he was 102. Her father, the woman said, was relating what had been told him by one Eagle Woman.[6]

Included in Eastman's report was a transcription prepared by Indian agent James I. Patten of an 1877 census roll of inhabitants of the reservation. Where the roll said simply "Bazil's Mother," Patten interpolated "Sacajawea."[7]

Eastman cited Brackenridge's journal of his 1811 journey up the Missouri, the relevant portion of which read in full:

"We had on board a Frenchman named Charbonneau, with his wife, an Indian woman of the Snake nation, both of whom had accompanied Lewis and Clark to the Pacific, and were of great service. The woman, a good creature, was of a mild and gentle disposition, greatly attached to the whites, whose manners and dress she tries to imitate, but she had become sickly, and longed

125

to revisit her native country; her husband, also, who had spent many years among the Indians, had become weary of civilized life."[8]

The words "with his wife" certainly suggest that Toussaint, although he had more than one wife at times, had only one with him on the trip. And Brackenridge, although he did not name this wife, said that both she and her husband accompanied Lewis and Clark to the Pacific. Eastman omitted this part of the journal entry in quoting it, and concluded that "the Shoshone woman who died at Fort Manuel, was Otter Woman, the other Shoshone wife of Charbonneau." Hebard herself, however, in her 1907 article, said, "In 1811, Brackinridge [sic] states that Sacajawea and Charbonneau were seen on the Missouri River."[9]

Grave marker in the "Sacajawea Cemetery" on the Wind River Reservation near Fort Washakie, Wyoming, where Grace Hebard and her followers believe Sacagawea is buried. (Photo by Joyce Miller Nelson)

Since the journals are clear that Sacagawea was the only woman on the expedition, the conclusion seems inescapable that she was the "his wife" referred to by Brackenridge. And John C. Luttig's journal entry of December 20, 1812, said "this Evening the wife of Charbonneau a Snake Squaw, died of a putrid fever." Again, it is "the wife," not "a wife." Toussaint could have had another wife at Fort Manuel, but there is no evidence he did. Luttig thought well of the woman whose death he recorded, describing her as "a good woman—the best in the fort."[10]

Luttig's journal was first published in 1920, thirteen years after Hebard's article, but thirteen years before her 1933 book "Sacajawea." In the book, she enlarged on the thesis that it was Otter Woman who died at Fort Manuel, and concluded that it "must be accepted on the basis not only of the tribal tradition, but of other evidence that corroborates that tradition so strikingly that its truth cannot be questioned."[11]

The remaining piece of contemporaneous documentary evidence on the subject came to light in the 1950s, after Hebard's death, when Dale L. Morgan of the Bancroft Library was examining a collection of William Clark's papers owned by a Chicago collector. On the cover of an account book covering the years 1825 to 1828, Clark had compiled a list of the expedition members, noting whether each was still living. Beside the name "Se car ja we au," he wrote, "Dead." It seems unlikely that Clark, who befriended Sacagawea and became her children's guardian, would not have known whether she was still living.[12]

Doubters have searched the Fort Manuel area and found no grave that could be identified as Sacagawea's. In reply, Indian ethnologists have pointed out that the Hidatsas among whom she lived often placed their dead on raised platforms in the woods rather than burying them.[13]

The final section of Hebard's book followed the career of Jean Baptiste Charbonneau up to the arrival of the Mormon Battalion in California. It made no mention of his service at Mission San Luis Rey, his Gold Rush experiences, or his residence in the Auburn area. Instead, it said that from 1852 until his death in 1885, he lived on the Wind River Reservation.

According to this theory, the J. B. Charbonneau who was found near Auburn by the census takers and listed in the city director as clerking at the Orleans Hotel, and who died at Inskip Station, was a different J. B. Charbonneau. Possibly. The 1860 census roll gave the name of the Secret Ravine Charbonneau as fifty-seven. As Baptiste was born in February, 1805, he would have been fifty-five in 1860. The Owyhee Avalanche obituary said the Inskip Station Charbonneau was sixty-three at his death in 1866, again just two years older than Baptiste would have been. The Idaho newspaper said the man who died at Inskip Station was born in St. Louis, which, although inaccurate, is consistent with Baptiste's St. Louis upbringing. It did not mention Lewis and Clark, but did say the deceased had been a guide for the Mormon Battalion and resided in Placer County, California. The *Placer Herald* obituary did not give J. B. Charbonneau's age, but said he was "born in the western wilds," came to California with the Mormon Battalion and panned for gold in the company of Jim Beckwourth. It said nothing of Lewis and Clark. Neither obituary mentioned San Luis Rey, where a man who signed his name "J. B. Charbonneau" and had been a guide to the Mormon Battalion was appointed alcalde to serve under his friend Captain Hunter.[14]

There was on the Wind River Reservation a Shoshone Indian named Bat-tez, who died in 1885 and was identified by Hebert as Jean Baptiste Charbonneau. Bat-tez was described as "a man of little force or importance" in the tribe, a heavy drinker, with a limited vocabulary in English. Hebard dismissed the strong contrast with descriptions of Baptiste in his prime by saying, "Culture that is only a veneering is easily rubbed off by constant association with uneducated Indians and illiterate whites."[15]

Writing of the adopted son Bazil, Hebard relied on a sentence attributed to the Lewis and Clark Journals saying that during the party's meeting with the Shoshones Sacagawea found that her family's few survivors included "a small boy who was immediately adopted by her." The child is identified as the son of her eldest sister, who had died. This passage is found in the 1814 account written by Nicholas Biddle, which was advertised as based on Lewis and Clark's journals along with information from other members of the expedition. The words are repeated in the 1902 edition by James K. Hosmer, which, like that of Biddle, paraphrases the journals and elaborates on them. Hebard's footnotes and an outline she prepared before writing the book show that she relied on the Hosmer edition. The 1904 edition by Reuben Gold Thwaites, a transcription of the journals themselves, makes no mention of any adopted child. Nor does the more recent definitive edition by Gary Moulton. If there was an adopted child, Hebard acknowledged that what happened to him is a puzzle. If a second child was taken along on the expedition, neither Lewis nor Clark nor any of the three enlisted men who kept journals mentions him.[16]

Although Hebard's conclusions still have supporters, their number has waned. In a 1941 article listing six outstanding American women, Pulitzer Prize-winning historian James Truslow Adams included Sacagawea, but indicated the date of her death by a question mark. And when Wyoming Senator Mike Enzi urged placing the image of Sacagawea on the dollar coin in 1998, he took a politically circumspect stance, acknowledging that there was dispute about where and when she died, but adding that whichever version is correct, her story is "an inspiration to all Americans."[17]

The narrow road cuts off from U.S. 287 at Fort Washakie on the Wind River Reservation and passes the crumbling mission where John Roberts served sixty-six years as missionary to the Shoshones.

Around a bend it reaches the "Sacajawea Cemetery," where a dirt path leads through the white crosses of the Shoshone dead to a granite pillar erected in 1963 by Wyoming's Daughters of the American Revolution to replace one installed years earlier.

The legend reads, as it did on the first tablet: "Sacajawea. Died April 9, 1884. A Guide with the Lewis and Clark Expedition, 1805-1806, Identified, 1907, by the Rev. John Roberts, who Officiated at Her Burial."[18]

By its side is another marker, "Dedicated to the Memory of Jean Baptiste Charbonneau, Papoose of the Lewis and Clark Expedition." The Indians say the man known as Bat-tez was buried in a gorge in the Wind River Mountains a few miles to the West.[19]

Like the other graves, the Sacajawea site is decorated with artificial flowers. There are also a string of beads, a cross and a scattering of pennies and nickels. There are few trees around, mostly sagebrush and prairie grass.

Each summer, tourists flock to this forlorn spot, following the AAA tour book for Wyoming or other directions, to see the grave of the woman identified as Lewis and Clark's guide.

The contemporaneous documentary evidence, while not conclusive, clearly indicates that Sacagawea died at Fort Manuel on a fine December evening in 1812. Barring some elaborate imposture, it seems that the man who died at Inskip Station must have been Jean Baptiste Charbonneau. Nevertheless, there are those who believe that tribal tradition outweighs the musty documents of scholars. Even those of us who do not subscribe to this somewhat mystical view should perhaps consider the words of the psychologist-philosopher William James: "To no one type of mind is it given to discern the totality of truth."[20]

Of Shakespeare's rather fanciful depiction of the career of England's King Richard III, it has been said that the chronicles of a country are "an interwoven tapestry of history and legend."[21]

The traces of Toussaint Charbonneau and Sacagawea and their son Jean Baptiste are found in the journals of Meriwether Lewis and William Clark, of Francis Chardon and Colonel Cooke, and of Henry Brackenridge and John C. Luttig. They are found in the baptismal records of a tiny church in St. Louis, in the official correspondence of Indian agent Joshua Pilcher, and in the records of frontier justice at Mission San Luis Rey. They are found in census rolls and a city directory and newspaper obituaries.

They are also found here, in a bleak cemetery on the Wind River Reservation.

The Charbonneau family is part of American history, part of American myth—of stories, false and true, that will not die.

Notes

Introduction

1. John E. Sunder, Joshua Pilcher: *Fur Trader and Indian Agent* (Norman: University of Oklahoma Press, 1968), 140-41, 143, 145, 147-48, 150; Louise Barry, ed., "William Clark's Diary, May, 1826-February, 1831: Part One," *Kansas Historical Quarterly*, February, 1948, 16-17. The Army withheld Clark's commission as a captain, and he was technically a lieutenant, but his pay was the same as Lewis's, the two addressed each other as captain and both are referred to as captains in the journals. See Donald Jackson, ed., *Letters of the Lewis and Clark Expedition with Related Documents, 1783-1854*, 2d ed. (Urbana: University of Illinois Press, 1978), I, 173, 179.

2. Sunder, 122, 144-48; Jackson II, 648-49; LeRoy R. Hafen, ed., *The Mountain Men and the Fur Trade of the Far West: Biographical Sketches of the Participants by Scholars of the Subject* (Glendale, Calif.: Arthur H. Clark, 1965), 217.

Chapter One: The Meeting

1. Gary E. Moulton, ed., *The Journals of the Lewis & Clark Expedition* (Lincoln: University of Nebraska Press, 1987) III, 228-29; Annie Heloise Abel, ed., *Chardon's Journals at Fort Clark* (Pierre: Department of History, State of South Dakota, 1932), 14, 31; Ernest Staples Osgood, ed., *The Field Notes of Captain William Clark, 1803-1805* (New Haven: Yale University Press, 1964) 172.

2. Moulton, IX, 93; Carol Lynn MacGregor, *The Journals of Patrick Gass: Member of the Lewis and Clark Expedition* (Missoula, Mont.: Mountain Press Publishing Company, 1997), 14-15; Osgood, 173.

3. Moulton III, 226-27.

4. Reuben Gold Thwaites, ed., *Early Western Travels, 1748-1846.* 32 vols. (Cleveland, Ohio: Arthur H. Clark, 1904), XXIII, 223; James P. Ronda, *Lewis and Clark among the Indians* (Lincoln: University of Nebraska Press, 1984), 70-73.

5. Donald Jackson, *Letters of the Lewis and Clark Expedition with Related Documents, 1783-1854,* 2d ed. (Urbana: University of Illinois Press, 1978), I, 57-66.

6. Jackson, I, 37-38, n40, 115-119, 123.

7. Peter C. Newman, *Company of Adventurers: The Story of the Hudson's Bay Company* (Hammondsworth, Middlesex, England: Penguin Books, 1985), I, 247-48.

8. Moulton, III, 3, 228.

9. Jackson, II, 378; Charles Larpenteur, *Forty Years a Fur Trader on the Upper Missouri* (Lincoln: University of Nebraska Press, 1989), 72-73; Osgood, 174.

10. Moulton, IV, 11; Moulton, XI, 8; Moulton IX, 95-97.

11. John Bakeless, *Lewis & Clark: Partners in Discovery* (New York: W. Morrow, 1947), 2, 22; MacGregor, 8.

12. John Upton Terrell, *Furs by Astor* (New York: W. Morrow, 1963), 64-75; Moulton, III, n228-29.

13. Raymond W. Wood and Robert D. Thiessen, eds., *Early Fur Trade on the Northern Plains* (Norman: University of Oklahoma Press, 1985), 42-46; Thwaites, XXIII, 230, 276, 357; Wood and Thiessen, 6; Elwyn B. Robinson, *History of North Dakota* (Lincoln: University of Nebraska Press, 1966), 19, 21; John C. Luttig, *Journal of a Fur-Trading Expedition on the Upper Missouri, 1812-1813,* ed. by Stella M. Drumm (reprint, New York: Argosy-Antiquarian Press, 1964), 136; Hilde Beaty, "Louis and Toussaint Charbonneau," *Families*, February, 1987; A. P. Nasatir, ed. *Before Lewis and Clark: Documents Illustrating the History of the Missouri, 1785-1804* (St. Louis: St. Louis Historical Documents Foundation, 1952), II, 831.

14. Russell Reid, "Sakakawea," *North Dakota History,* July, 1963, 101-03; Ronda, 256; Reuben Gold Thwaites, *Original Journals of the Lewis and Clark Expedition, 1804-1806* (New York: Dodd, Mead, 1904), I, 219; Sylvia Van Kirk, *Many Tender Ties: Women in Fur Trade Society, 1670-1870* (Norman: University of Oklahoma Press, 1980), 36-37; Brigham D.

Madsen, *The Lemhi: Sacajawea's People* (Caldwell, Idaho: Caxton Printers, 1979), 25-26. Abel, 271; "Maraje of Toussaint Charbonneau," *Dictinnain Hishrique Des Canadiens* (Quebec, 1908), excerpt in Grace Raymond Hebard Papers, 1829-1947, Accession Number 40008, Box Number 33, Folder Number 3, American Heritage Center, University of Wyoming; Donna J. Kessler, *The Making of Sacagawea: A Euro-American Legend* (Tuscaloosa: University of Alabama Press, 1996), 78-79; Moulton V, 8-9, IX, 192.

15. "Peak Named for Squaw Who Aided Lewis, Clark," unidentified newspaper clipping, Nov. 23, 1930, Grace Raymond Hebard Papers, Box Number 56, Folder Number 8; Toledo Choral Society program, March 13, 1931, Hebard papers, Box 44, Folder 10; Ronald W. Taber, "Sacagawea and the Suffragettes: An Interpretation of a Myth," *Pacific Northwest Quarterly*, January, 1967, 7-9.

16. George Creel, "Path of Empire," *Collier's*, April 17, 1926, 7-8; John Logan Allen, *Passage through the Garden: Lewis and Clark and the Image of the American Northwest* (Urbana: University of Illinois Press, 1975), 96-98, 147-49, 154-55.

17. Jackson, I, 61-66; Bernard De Voto, *Across the Wide Missouri* (Boston: Houghton Mifflin, 1947), 98, 101-102; Wood and Thiessen, 117; Roy W. Meyer, *The Village Indians of the Upper Missouri: The Mandans, Hidatsas, and Arikaras* (Lincoln: University of Nebraska Press, 1977), 68; Moulton, V, 133-34; Thwaites, *Early Western Travels*, XXIII, 265; DeVoto, 173-74.

18. Irving W. Anderson, "Sacajawea, Sacagawea, Sakakawea?," *South Dakota History*, Fall, 1978, 304-10; Irving W. Anderson and Blanche Schroer, "Sacagawea: Her Name and Her Destiny," *We Proceeded On*, November, 1999, 8; Ronda, 256-57; Reid, 101, 103; Irving W. Anderson, *A Charbonneau Family Portrait: Biographical Sketches of Sacagawea, Jean Baptiste, and Toussaint Charbonneau* (Astoria, Ore.: Clatsop Historical Association, 1992), 5-6; Blake Nicholson, Associated Press Writer, "'Sakakawea' spelling change considered by tribes council," *Casper Star-Tribune*, August 16, 2002, B3, and "Sacagawea or Sakakawea: Debate over Indian woman's name goes another round," *Santa Fe New Mexican*, October 29, 2002, B4; Amy Mossett, tourism director, Three Affiliated Tribes Business Council, author's telephone interview; Claudia Berg, Museum

and Education Division director, State Historical Society of North Dakota, author's telephone interview.

19. Jackson, I, 315, 369; Elliot Coues, ed. *History of the Expedition under the Command of Lewis and Clark* (New York: Francis P. Harper, 1893), I, n189-90; Thwaites, *Original Journals*, VI, n32-33; Donna J. Kessler, *The Making of Sacagawea: A Euro-American Legend* (Tuscaloosa: University of Alabama Press, 1996), 218, n11; James Kendall Hosmer, ed., *Gass's Journal of the Lewis and Clark Expedition* (Chicago: A. C. McClurg, 1904), xxxv.

20. David Meriwether, *My Life in the Mountains and on the Plains: The Newly Discovered Autobiography,* edited by Robert A. Griffen (Norman: University of Oklahoma Press, 1965), xv, 78.

21. Wood and Thiessen, 16, 42-47, 51; Richard Edward Oglesby, *Manuel Lisa and the Opening of the Missouri Fur Trade* (Norman: University of Oklahoma Press, 1963), 120-21; Hiram Martin Chittenden, *The American Fur Trade of the Far West* (Lincoln: University of Nebraska Press, 1986), I, 367.

22. Jackson, II, 501-06; Abel, 271; Van Kirk, 46, 52; Elwyn B. Robinson, *History of North Dakota* (Lincoln; University of Nebraska Press, 1966), 47.

23. Wood and Thiessen, 47; Ottoson, 154-55; Elliott Coues, ed., *New Light on the Early History of the Greater Northwest: The Manuscript Journals of Alexander Henry, Fur Trader of the Northwest Company, and of David Thompson, Official Geographer and Explorer of the Same Company* (New York: Francis P. Harper, 1897), III, n50; Oglesby, 49, 153-54; Moulton, III, n228-29; Moulton, III, 224; Thwaites, *Early Travels*, XXIII, 221; Bakeless, 155.

24. Thwaites, *Early Travels*, XXIII, 254-55, 269-71, 367; W. Raymond Wood and Margot Liberty, *Anthropology on the Great Plains* (Lincoln: University of Nebraska Press, 1950), 291; Moulton, III, 228; John C. Ewers, et al, *Views of a Vanishing Frontier* (Omaha: Center for Western Studies/ Joslyn Art Museum, 1984), 62.

25. Dayton Duncan, *Out West: An American Journey* (New York: Viking, 1987), 182-83; Moulton, III, 228, 249, Allen L. Truax, "Manuel Lisa and His North Dakota Trading Post," *North Dakota Historical Quarterly*, July, 1928, n243; Meyer, 46.

26. Thwaites, *Early Travels*, XXII, 357; Ottoson, 157.

Chapter Two: Winter

1. W. Raymond Wood and Thomas D. Thiessen, eds. *Early Fur Trade on the Northern Plains* (Norman: University of Oklahoma Press, 1985), 13.

2. Wood and Thiessen, 136-37.

3. Gary E. Moulton, ed., *The Journals of the Lewis & Clark Expedition* (Lincoln: University of Nebraska Press, 1993-97), III, 241, n241-42.

4. Wood and Thiessen, 137; Moulton, III, 250, 262; Dennis R. Ottoson, "Toussaint Charbonneau: A Most Durable Man," *South Dakota History*, Spring, 1976, 158.

5. Wood and Thiessen, 138; Moulton, III, 242; James P. Ronda, *Lewis and Clark Among the Indians* (Lincoln: University of Nebraska Press, 1984), 94-95.

6. Wood and Thiessen, 140; Moulton, III, 244-47; Ronda, 95-98.

7. Wood and Thiessen, 140-41.

8. Wood and Thiessen, 141.

9. Ibid.

10. Wood and Thiessen, 12, 142-43.

11. Moulton, III, 260.

12. Moulton, III, 261; Carol Lynn MacGregor, ed., *The Journals of Patrick Gass, Member of the Lewis and Clark Expedition* (Missoula, Mont.: Mountain Press Publishing Company, 1997) 79.

13. Wood and Thiessen, 144-45.

14. Moulton, III, 272, 273.

15. Moulton, IX, 108-09, X, 69, n70.

16. Moulton, III, 285-86, 290-91.

17. Moulton, III, n205, 277, 284.

18. Moulton, III, 291, X, 72; Ottoson, 159; MacGregor, 82-83; Helen Crawford, "Sakakawea," *North Dakota Historical Quarterly*, April, 1927, 5.

19. Ernest Staples Osgood, ed., *The Field Notes of Captain William Clark, 1803-1805* (New Haven: Yale University Press, 1964), 176; M. O. Skarsten, *George Drouillard: Hunter and Interpreter for Lewis and Clark and Fur Trader, 1807-1810* (Glendale, Calif.: Arthur H. Clark, 1964), 42.

20. Ottoson, 159-60; Elliot Coues, ed., *History of the Expedition under the*

Command of Lewis and Clark, 1804-1806 (New York: Dodd, Mead, 1904), I, 42.

21. Moulton, III, 4, n154, X, 123-25.

22. Moulton, III, 327, n327-28, IV, 9; Charles G. Clarke, *The Men of the Lewis and Clark Expedition* (Glendale, Calif.: Arthur H. Clark, 1970), 38; Osgood, 185.

23. Moulton, IV, 7-11.

Chapter Three: Against the Current

1. Donald Jackson, ed., *Letters of the Lewis and Clark Expedition with Related Documents, 1783-1854*, 2d. ed. (Urbana: University of Illinois Press, 1978), I, 222-23; Richard Edward Oglesby, *Manuel Lisa and the Opening of the Missouri Fur Trade* (Norman: University of Oklahoma Press, 1963), 43-44; Gary E. Moulton, ed., *The Journals of the Lewis and Clark Expedition* (Lincoln: University of Nebraska Press, 1983-1997), II, 302, 304, n373, 375, 377-78, 445, 458; Reuben Gold Thwaites, *Original Journals of the Lewis and Clark Expedition, 1804-1806* (New York: Dodd, Mead, 1904), VII, 34, 36-37, 54, 60; M. O. Skarsten, *George Drouillard: Hunter and Interpreter for Lewis and Clark and Fur Trader, 1807-1810* (Glendale, Calif.: Arthur H. Clark, 1964), 97.

2. Moulton, IV, 13.

3. Moulton, IV, 29-30.

4. Moulton, IV, 38, 39, IX, 131; Dennis R. Ottoson, "Toussaint Charbonneau, a Most Durable Man," *South Dakota History*, Spring, 1976, 161.

5. Moulton, IV, 52, 88, 89, 128, IX, 139; Ottoson, 162.

6. Moulton, IV, 131; John Charles Frémont, *The Life of Col. John Charles Frémont and His Narratives of Explorations and Adventures in Kansas, Nebraska, Oregon and California* (New York: Miller, Orton and Mulligan, 1856), 92.

7. Moulton, IV, 2, 152-54; Thwaites, *Original Journals*, II, n197.

8. Skarsten, 321-22.

9. Carol Lynne MacGregor, ed. *The Journals of Patrick Gass: Member of the Lewis and Clark Expedition* (Missoula, Mont.: Mountain Press Publishing Company, 1997), 94; Moulton, IV, 153.

10. Moulton, IV, 156-58, 171, n175, IX, 148, 156-58.

11. Moulton, IV, 158-62.

12. Moulton, IV, 84-85, 151, 154-55, IX, 147-48.

13. Moulton, IV, 276, 277, 279, 281, 287, 294-95, 297, 299; Paul Russell Cutright, "I Gave Him Barks and Saltpeter." *American Heritage*, December, 1963, 59, 96-97.

14. Moulton, IV, 279.

15. Moulton, IV, 294, 297, 301: Dennis R. Ottoson, "Toussaint Charbonneau, a Most Durable Man." *South Dakota History*, Spring, 1976, 162.

16. Moulton, IV, 299-301, 303.

17. Moulton, IV, 306, 309, 317-18.

18. Moulton, IV, 325-26.

19. Moulton, IV, 326-28.

20. Moulton, IV, 326-32.

21. Moulton, IV 3, 340-43.

22. Moulton, IV, 341-43, IX, 176-77, X, 107-108, XI, 206; Olin D. Wheeler, *The Trail of Lewis and Clark, 1804-1904* (New York: G. P. Putnam's Sons, 1904), I, 331-32.

23. Moulton, IV, 343.

24. Moulton, IV, 343, XI, 215.

25. Moulton, IV, 350, 354.

26. Moulton, IV, 378, 415-17, 418, 422, 427, 428, 431, 432-33, IX, 183, XI, 242-43; Charles G. Clarke, *The Men of the Lewis and Clark Expedition: A Biographical Roster of the Fifty-One Members and a Composite Diary of Their Activities from all Known Sources* (Glendale, Calif.: Arthur H. Clark, 1970), 48-49; Ottoson, 163.

27. Moulton, IV, 428,

28. Moulton, V, 8-9, IX, 190; Ottoson, 163.

29. Moulton, V, 17-18, 24, X, 119.

30. Earle R. Forrest, *Patrick Gass: Lewis and Clark's Last Man* (Independence, Pa.: Mrs. A.M. Painter, 1950), 8; John J. Peebles, "Rugged Waters: Trails and Campsites of Lewis and Clark in the Salmon River Country" *Idaho Yesterdays*, Summer, 1964, 4; Moulton, V, 42, 44-45.

31. Moulton, V, 52-54.

32. Moulton, V, 68-71, n72, 88; Skarsten, 126; Bernard DeVoto, *The Course of Empire* (Boston: Houghton Mifflin, 1952), 140.

33. Moulton, V, 73-77, 78-79.

34. Skarsten, 130; Brigham D. Madsen, *The Lemhi: Sacagawea's People* (Caldwell, Idaho: Caxton Printers, 1979), 22-27.

35. Moulton, V, 80-83

36. Moulton, V, 98-100.

37. Moulton, IV, 109.

38. Moulton, V, 109-15, 120, IX, 204-206, XI, 283-85; Nicholas Biddle, *History of the Expedition under the Command of Captains Lewis and Clarke: A Complete Reprint of the Biddle Edition of 1814* (New York: Allerton Book Co., 1972); II, 72-74; MacGregor, 239.

39. Moulton, V, 114.

40. Moulton, V, 120.

41. Moulton, V, 111-13.

Chapter Four: Over the Top

1. Gary E. Moulton, ed. *The Journals of the Lewis & Clark Expedition* (Lincoln: University of Nebraska Press, 1983-1997), V, 113, 115, 131, 143.

2. Moulton, V, 117.

3. Moulton, V, 162-63.

4. Moulton, V, 120.

5. Moulton, V, 120, 122.

6. Moulton, V. 158, 165.

7. Moulton, V, 165-66.

8. Moulton, V, 175-77, IX, 212-14, XI, 287-88; Bob Moore, "A Closer Look at the Uniform Coats of the Lewis and Clark Expedition," *We Proceeded On*, November, 1998, 4; Loren M. Gibbons, "All Them Horses and One Poor Mule," *We Proceeded On*, August, 2002, 29.

9. Moulton, V, 175, 183, 188,

10. Moulton, IX, 218, X, 137, XI 293, 296, 298-99, 300, 301; Ladd Hamilton, *Snowbound* (Pullman: Washington State University Press, 1997), 26; Gibbons, 29.

11. Moulton, V, 189, IX, 219, XI, 301, 303, 322; James P. Ronda, *Lewis*

and Clark among the Indians (Lincoln: University of Nebraska Press, 1984), 156; Ronda, 156-57.

12. Moulton, V, 219-23, 233, XI, 327-28; XI, 303.

13. Moulton, V, 249, 256, X, 132; Carol Lynn MacGregor, ed., *The Journals of Patrick Gass, Member of the Lewis and Clark Expedition* (Missoula, Mont.: Mountain Press Publishing Company, 1997), 137.

14. Moulton, V, 255, 258, 268, 306; James Alexander Thom, "Life among the Nee Mee Poo," *We Proceeded On*, May, 2000, 27.

15. Moulton, V, 277-78.

16. Moulton, V, 304-05, IX, 242, XI, 356.

17. Moulton, V, 345, VI, 10, 12, 13, n14, 16, 21, 23-26, 33-35, XI, 381.

Chapter Five: Fort Clatsop

1. Gary E. Moulton, ed., *The Journals of the Lewis & Clark Expedition* (Lincoln: University of Nebraska Press, 1983-1997), VI, 60-61, IX, 254-55, XI, 394-95.

2. Moulton, VI, 62, 65-67, VII, n221-22, IX 254-55, X, 175-76, n175.

3. Moulton, XI, 396-97.

4. Moulton, VI, 73, IX, 255-56, X, 176, XI, 396-97; Bob Moore, "A Closer Look at the Uniform Coats of the Lewis and Clark Expedition," *We Proceeded On*, November, 1998, 4.

5. Moulton, VI, 83-84, n186.

6. Moulton, VI, 92-93, 108-09, 244, 279, IX, 257-60.

7. Moulton, V, 127, VI, 137, IX, 105-06, 206, 262, X, 184, XI, 113.

8. Moulton, VI, 171, IX 262-63, 264-66, XI, 410.

9. Moulton, VI, 171-73.

10. Moulton, VI, 175-76, 178.

11. Moulton VI, 182; Glen Kirkpatrick, "The Rediscovery of Clark's Point of View," *We Proceeded On*, February, 1999, 28-30.

12. Moulton, VI, 183, XI 87-88.

13. Moulton VI, 156-57, 180-84.

14. James P. Ronda, *Lewis and Clark among the Indians* (Lincoln: University of Nebraska Press, 1984), 210; Elliot Coues, *History of the Expedition under the Command of Lewis and Clark* (New York: Francis P. Harper, 1893), II, 779.

15. Moulton V, 217, VI, 253-54.

16. Moulton VI, 428, IX, 277-78; Ronda, 211-12.

17. Moulton IX, 279-800.

Chapter Six: Homeward Bound

1. Gary E. Moulton, ed. *The Journals of the Lewis & Clark Expedition* (Lincoln: University of Nebraska Press, 1983-1997), VI, 84, n86.; Donald Jackson, ed., *Letters of the Lewis and Clark Expedition with Related Documents, 1783-1854*, 2d. ed., Urbana: University of Illinois Press, 1978), I, 315-16; Moulton VII, 119, 121; Irving W. Anderson, *A Charbonneau Family Portrait: Biographical Sketches of Sacagawea, Jean Baptiste, and Toussaint Charbonneau* (Astoria, Ore.: Fort Clatsop Historical Association, 1992). Reprinted from *American West Magazine*, March-April, 1980, 7-8;

2. John Logan Allen, *Passage through the Garden: Lewis and Clark and the Image of the American Northwest* (Urbana: University of Illinois Press, 1975), n275, 355.

3. Moulton, VII, 74, 124-139, IX, 292-95; James P. Ronda, *Lewis and Clark among the Indians* (Lincoln: University of Nebraska Press, 1984), 217-19; Stephen E. Ambrose, *Undaunted Courage: Meriwether Lewis, Thomas Jefferson, and the Opening of the American West* (New York: Simon & Schuster, 1996), 346.

4. Ronda, 219-20; Moulton, VII, 155-57; M. O. Skarsten, *George Drouillard: Hunter and Interpreter for Lewis and Clark and Fur Trader, 1807-1810* (Glendale, Calif.: Arthur H. Clark, 1964), 186.

5. Moulton, VII, 158-62.

6. Moulton, VII, 173-74, X, 223.

7. Moulton, VII, 177-79, IX, 313, X, 230, 233, n237; Ronda, 228; Skarsten, 195.

8. Moulton, VII, 226-32; Ronda, 229.

9. Moulton, VII, 246-99; Carol Lynn McGregor, ed., *The Journals of Patrick Gass: Member of the Lewis and Clark Expedition* (Missoula, Mont.: Mountain Press Publishing Co., 1997), 189, 190.

10. Moulton, VII, 308-10.

11. Eldon G. Chuinard, *Only One Man Died: The Medical Aspects of the Lewis and Clark Expedition* (Glendale, Calif.: Arthur H. Clark, 1979), 370,

374-76; Paul Russell Cutright, "I Gave Him Barks and Saltpeter," *American Heritage*, December, 1963, 97; Moulton, VII, 278-94; McGregor, 190.

12. Moulton, VII, 285-94, 330-31.

13. Moulton, VII, 343-45, 346-47, X, 236-37.

14. Moulton, VIII, 1, 10-11, 32-34, 48, 68.

15. Moulton, VIII, 1, 74, 161-62, IX, 330: Milo M. Quaife, ed., *The Journals of Captain Meriwether Lewis and Sergeant John Ordway* (Madison: State Historical Society of Wisconsin, 1916), n371-72.

16. Moulton, VIII, 1, 179-180, n180, 184-87, n188.

17. Moulton, VIII, 200.

18. Moulton, VIII, 202-04; Charles G. Clarke, *The Men of the Lewis and Clark Expedition: A Biographical Roster of the Fifty-One Members and a Composite Diary of Their Activities from all Known Sources* (Glendale, Calif.: Arthur H. Clark, 1970), 49.

19. Moulton, VIII, 201-06.

20. Moulton, VIII, 209-11; Loren M. Hutton, "All Them Horses and One Poor Mule," *We Proceeded On*, August, 2002, 32.

21. Moulton, VIII, 210-11; Ambrose, 138; Charles G. Clarke, *The Men of the Lewis and Clark Expedition* (Glendale, Calif.: Arthur H. Clark, 1970), 64.

22. Moulton, VIII, 3, 213-14.

23. Moulton, VIII, 217-19.

24. Moulton, VIII, 224-5, n228, 284; Anderson, 14.

25. Moulton, VIII, 3, 272-3, 275, 281-283; Reuben Gold Thwaites, ed., *Original Journals of the Lewis and Clark Expedition, 1804-1806* (New York: Dodd, Mead, 1905), 318-19.

26. Moulton, VIII, 289-95, 298, 303-305; Ronda 245, 246-47.

27. Moulton, VIII, 303-305; Ronda 246.

28. Moulton, VIII, 305-306; Dennis R. Ottoson, "Toussaint Charbonneau, a Most Durable Man," *South Dakota History*, Spring, 1976. 106.

29. Jackson, I, 368-69.

30. Ottoson, 167; Jackson, I, 315-16; LeRoy R. Hafen, *The Mountain Men and the Fur Trade of the Far West: Biographical Sketches of the Participants by Scholars of the Subject* (Glendale, Calif.: Arthur H. Clark, 1965),

208; Rita Cleary, "Charbonneau Reconsidered," *We Proceeded On*, February, 2000, 18-23; Jackson, I, 315-16.

31. Jackson, I, 315-16.

32. Ibid.

33. Ibid.

34. Ibid.

35. Ibid; Dan Slosberg, "Music, Myth, and Pierre Cruzztte." *We Proceeded On*, February, 2000, 18-23.

36. Jackson, I, 315-16.

37. Moulton, VIII, 305-306.

Chapter Seven: Afterward

1. Richard Edward Oglesby, *Manuel Lisa and the Opening of the Missouri FurTrade* (Norman: University of Oklahoma Press, 1963), 106.

2. Donald Jackson, ed., *Letters of the Lewis and Clark Expedition with Related Documents, 1783-1854*, 2d. ed. (Urbana: University of Illinois Press, 1978), II, 378-82; *The Debates and Proceedings in the Congress of the United States*: Ninth Congress-Second Session (Washington: Gales and Seaton, 1852), 103.

3. Moore, Bob, "Pompey's Baptism," *We Proceeded On*, February, 2000, 10-17.

4. Oglesby, 68-69, 109; Jackson, II, 501-506; John C. Luttig, *Journal of a Fur-trading Expedition on the Upper Missouri, 1812-1813*, Stella M. Drumm, ed. (St. Louis: Missouri Historical Society, 1975), 138.

5. Oglesby, 109; Irving W. Anderson, "Probing the Riddle of the Bird Woman," *Montana, Magazine of Western History*, Autumn, 1973, 12-13.

6. Hiram Martin Chittenden, *Fur Trade of the Far West* (Lincoln: University of Nebraska Press, 1986), 127; Oglesby, 23-24; William E. Foley and David C. Rice, *The First Chouteaus: River Barons of Early St. Louis* (Urbana: University of Illinois Press, 1983), 60-61.

7. John Upton Terrell, *Furs by Astor* (New York: William Morrow, 1963), 32-35.

8. Oglesby, 109; Thwaites, VI, 32-33

9. Terrell, 143-49, 167-74; Allen L. Truax, "Manuel Lisa and His North Dakota Trading Post," *North Dakota Historical Quarterly*, July, 1928, 241-42.

10. Thwaites, VI, 43; Terrell, 190.

11. Truax, 237, 241-43, 243n.

12. Truax, 239; Doane Robinson, "A Sioux Indian View of the Last War with England," *South Dakota Historical Collections*, 1910, 309, 401, and "South Dakota and the War of 1812," *South Dakota Historical Collections*, XII, 88, 89, 93.

13. Luttig, 13-14, 84, 137; D. Robinson, "South Dakota and the War," 89.

14. Luttig, 78-79, 83.

15. Luttig, 92-93.

16. Luttig, 106.

17. Luttig, 121, 124.

18. D. Robinson, "South Dakota and the War," 90-91; Luttig, 126-28.

19. D. Robinson, "South Dakota and the War," 91; Ottoson, 173; Schroer, 41.

20. Hebard, 161, 222; Jackson, II, n640; Irving W. Anderson, *A Charbonneau Family Portrait: Biographical Sketches of Sacagawea, Jean Baptiste, and Toussaint Charbonneau* (Fort Clatsop Historical Association, 1992, reprinted from *American West Magazine*, March-April, 1980), 16; Ottoson, 170; Anderson, "Probing the Riddle of the Bird Woman," *Montana, the Magazine of Western History*, Autumn, 1973, 15.

21. Dale L. Morgan, ed. *The West of William H. Ashley, 1822-1838* (Denver: Old West Publishing Company, 1964), xlvii; William E. Foley and C. David Rice, *The First Chouteaus: River Barons of Early St. Louis* (Urbana: University of Illinois Press, 1983), 176.

Chapter Eight: Father and Son

1. American State Papers, Class II, Indian Affairs, Volume II, Accounts of Superintendent of Indian Affairs, 1822, Washington: 1834. Typed copy in Grace Raymond Hebard Papers, 1829-1947, Accession Number 40008, Box Number 33, Folder Number 3, American Heritage Center, University of Wyoming.

2. Donald Jackson, ed., *Letters of the Lewis and Clark Expedition with Related Documents, 1783-1854,* 2d. ed. (Urbana: University of Illinois Press, 1978), I, 315-16; Gary E. Moulton, ed., *The Journals of the Lewis & Clark*

Expedition (Lincoln: University of Nebraska Press, 1983-1997), VIII, 305-6.

3. American State Paper Papers, Class II, Indian Affairs, Volume II.

4. Leroy R. Hafen, ed., *The Mountain Men and the Fur Trade of the Far West: Biographical Sketches of the Participants by Scholars of the Subject* (Glendale, Calif., Arthur H. Clark, 1965), 208-9.

5. Anna Heloise Abel, ed., *Chardon's Journal at Fort Clark, 1834-1838* (Pierre: South Dakota Department of History, State University of South Dakota, 1932), 279.

6. David Meriwether, *My Life in the Mountains and on the Plains* (Norman: University of Oklahoma Press, 1965), 78.

7. Reuben Gold Thwaites, ed., *Early Western Travels, 1784-1846* (Cleveland: Arthur H. Clark, 1904), XIV, 182, 204.

8. Adrian R. Dunn, "A History of Old Fort Berthold," *North Dakota History*, October, 1963, 178-79; Hiram Martin Chittenden, *The American Fur Trade of the Far West* (Lincoln: University of Nebraska Press, 1986), 263-67; Elwyn B. Robinson, *History of North Dakota* (Lincoln: University of Nebraska Press, 1966), 84-85.

9. Dale L. Morgan, ed., *The West of William H. Ashley, 1822-1838* (Denver: Old West Publishing Company, 1964), 53, 56, 57, 73, 74.

Chapter Nine: At Home and Abroad

1. Paul Wilhelm, Duke of Wurttemberg, "First Journey to North America in the Years 1822 to 1824," translated by William G. Bek, *South Dakota History Collections*, 1938, 303-304.

2. L. C. Butscher, A Brief Biography of Prince Paul Wilhelm of Wurttemberg, unpublished manuscript, 1930, in Grace Raymond Hebard papers, American Heritage Center, University of Wyoming, Box 51, Folder 11, 1; LeRoy R. Hafen, *The Mountain Men and the Fur Trade of the Far West, Biographical Sketches of the Participants by Scholars of the Subject*, I, 211.

3. Paul Wilhelm, 232, 268.

4. Paul Wilhelm, 303-304.

5. Paul Wilhelm, 408-410; Friedrich Bauser, letter to Grace Raymond Hebard, June 27, 1933, Hebard papers, Box 51, Folder 4.

6. Hafen, *Mountain Men*, I, 209-11; Bauser, letter to Hebard.

7. Hafen, I, 210-11; Butscher, 5.

8. Rufus B. Sage, *Rocky Mountain Life or, Startling Scenes and Perilous Adventures in the Far West during an Expedition of Three Years* (Boston: Wentworth, 1858; Reprint, Lincoln: University of Nebraska Press, 1982), 205-7.

9. Dennis R. Ottoson, "Toussaint Charbonneau: A Most Durable Man," *South Dakota History*, Spring, 1976, 177; Dale L. Morgan, ed., *The West of William H. Ashley: The International Struggle for the Fur Trade of the Missouri, the Rocky Mountains, and the Columbia, with Exploration beyond the Continental Divide* (Denver: Old West Publishing Company, 1964), 73.

10. Russell Reed and Clell G. Cannon, eds., "Journal of the Atkinson-O'Fallon Expedition," *North Dakota Historical Quarterly*, October, 1929, 5-7; Elwyn B. Robinson, *History of North Dakota* (Lincoln: University of Nebraska Press, 1966), 84; James J. Holmberg, ed., *Dear Brother: Letters of William Clark to Jonathan Clark* (New Haven: Yale University Press, 2002), 260.

11. Reed and Cannon, 19, 21, 22; Charles J. Kappler, ed. *Indian Affairs. Laws and Treaties* (Washington: Government Printing Office, 1904), II, 242-44.

12. Kappler, 242.

13. Kappler, 243-44.

Chapter Ten: The Prince and the Frontiersman

1. Reuben Gold Thwaites, ed. *Early Western Travels, 1748-1846* (Cleveland: Arthur H. Clark, 1906), XXII, 344. 164-65.

2. O. A. Stevens, "Maximilian in North Dakota," 1833-34," *North Dakota History*, 1961, 164-65.

3. Erwin N. Thompson, *Fort Union Trading Post: Fur Trade Empire on the Upper Missouri* (Williston, N. Dak., Fort Union Association, 1994), 24.

4. Stevens, 164-65.

5. Stevens, 164-66.

6. Thompson, 24.

7. Thwaites, XXII, 344-46.

8. Alvera Berquist, "Karl Bodmer," *We Proceeded On*, May, 1999, 28; Thwaites, XXII, 350-51.

9. Thwaites, XXII, 365-57, 363, XXIII, 164-65.

10. Ibid., 217.

11. Ibid., 219.

12. Ibid., 219-21.

13. Thwaites, XXIV, 20-22, 20-29, 30-32.

14. Ibid., 22-24.

15. Thwaites, XXIV, 27-35; James P. Ronda, *Lewis and Clark among the Indians* (Lincoln: University of Nebraska Press, 1984), 107.

16. Thwaites, XXIV, 44, XXIII, 237.

17. Thwaites, XXIV, 52-53; Dale Morgan, ed., *The West of William Ashley* (Denver: Old West Publishing, 1964), 59.

18. Thwaites, XXIV, 64-67.

19. Ibid., 82-83.

Chapter Eleven: Glimpses of Baptiste

1. Warren Angus Ferris, *Life in the Rocky Mountains, 1830-1835* (Salt Lake City: Rocky Mountain Book Shop, 1940), 53-54.

2. Ferris, 54-59.

3. LeRoy R. Hafen, *The Mountain Men and the Fur Trade of the Far West: Biographical Sketches of the Participants by Scholars of the Subject* (Spokane, Wash.: Arthur H. Clark, 2000), I, 213, 317; Hafen, ed., "The W. M. Boggs Manuscript about Bent's Fort," *Colorado Magazine*, January, 1930, 66-67; Stanley Vestal, *Kit Carson: The Happy Warrior of the Old West* (Boston: Houghton Mifflin, 1931), 166, 169.

4. David Lavender, *Bent's Fort* (Garden City, N.Y.: Doubleday, 1954), 208-209; Elliott West, *The Way to the West: Essays on the Central Plains* (Albuquerque: University of New Mexico Press, 1995, 118; John Charles Frémont, *The Life of Col. John Charles Frémont and His Narratives of Exploration and Adventures in Kansas, Nebraska, Oregon and California* (New York: Miller, Orton and Mulligan, 1856), 106.

5. LeRoy R. Hafen and Francis Marion Young, *Fort Laramie and the Pageant of the West, 1834-1890* (Glendale, Calif.: Arthur H. Clark, 1938), 102-103; Harrison C. Dale, ed., "A Fragmentary Journal of William L.

Sublette," *Mississippi Valley Historical Review*, June, 1919, 108; Aubrey L. Haines, ed., *Osborne Russell's Journal of a Trapper* (Lincoln, University of Nebraska Press, 1967), 60.

Chapter Twelve: Desolation on the Missouri

1. Annie Heloise Abel, ed., *Chardon's Journal at Fort Clark, 1834-1839* (Pierre: Department of History, State of South Dakota, 1932), 7, 126.

2. Abel, xix, xx.

3. Abel, 11.

4. Abel, 123; Charles Larpenteur, *Forty Years a Fur Trader on the Upper Missouri* (Lincoln: University of Nebraska Press, 1989), n114.

5. Abel, 126-27.

6. Abel, 282.

7. Reuben Gold Thwaites, ed., *Early Western Travels, 1748-1846* (Cleveland: Arthur H. Clark, 1906), XXIII, 206; Larpenteur, 119-20; Abel, xxi.

8. Abel, 27, 31, 60.

9. Abel, 8, 18, 46, n313.

10. Abel, 12.

11. Abel, 14, 31.

12. Abel, xli, 53.

13. Abel, 52, 384-87.

14. Abel, 50, 69, 83, 90, 91.

15. Bernard DeVoto, *Across the Wide Missouri* (Boston: Houghton Mifflin, 1947), 272-76.

16. DeVoto, 277.

17. Grace Lee Nute, "James Dickson: A Filibuster in Minnesota in 1836," *Mississippi Valley Historical Review*, September, 1923, 128-131; DeVoto, 277; Abel, 104-5.

18. Abel, 117; DeVoto, 277.

19. Abel, 118; Frank H. Stewart, "Mandan and Hidatsa Villages in the Eighteenth and Nineteenth Centuries," *Plains Anthropology*, November, 1974, 292.

20. Abel, 120-23.

21. Abel, 124-5, 128.

22. Abel, 395; Erwin N. Thompson, *Fort Union Trading Post: Fur Trade*

Empire on the Upper Missouri (Williston, N. Dak.: Fort Union Association, 1994), 46; Hiram M. Chittenden, *The American Fur Trade of the West: a History of the Pioneer Trading Posts and Early Fur Companies of the Missouri Valley and the Rocky Mountains, and of the Overland Commerce with Santa Fe* (New York: F. P. Harper, 1902), 620.

23. Abel, 126, 129-31, 135; Elwyn B. Robinson, *History of North Dakota* (Lincoln: University of Nebraska, 1966), 98.

24. Abel, n351-52.

25. Abel, 132, 138, 140-41.

26. Abel, 146-50,

27. Larpenteur, 117-19.

28. Abel, 156-57.

29. John E. Sunder, *Joshua Pilcher: Fur Trader and Indian Agent* (Norman: University of Oklahoma Press, 1968), 125, 137-39.

30. Donald Jackson, *Letters of the Lewis and Clark Expedition with Related Documents, 1783-1854* (Urbana, University of Illinois Press, 1978), I, 64, 130; Eldon G. Chuinard, *Only One Man Died: The Medical Aspects of the Lewis and Clark Expedition* (Glendale, Calif.: Arthur H. Clark Company, 1979), 178-80.

31. Abel, n319.

32. Sunder, 139; Chittenden, II, 627; Thompson, 46; John Upton Terrell, *Black Robe: The Life of Pierre-Jean De Smet, Missionary, Explorer & Pioneer* (Garden City, N.Y.: Doubleday, 1964), 71.

33. Abel, 173; Sunder, 139-40.

34. William Shakespeare, *As You Like It*, Act II, Scene VII.

Chapter Thirteen: Westward Once More

1. Ralph P. Bieber, in collaboration with Averam B. Bender, ed., "Cooke's Journal of the March of the Mormon Battalion, 1846-1847," *Exploring Southwestern Trails, 1846-1854, Vol. VII of The Southwest Historical Series* (Glendale, Calif.: Arthur H. Clark, 1938), 23-24, 74.

2. Norma Baldwin Ricketts, *The Mormon Battalion: U.S. Army of the West, 1846-1848* (Logan: Utah State University Press, 1996), 1-2.

3. Ricketts, 3-5, 13-14.

4. Bieber, 25-27.

5. Grace Raymond Hebard, *Sacajawea: A Guide and Interpreter of the Lewis and Clark Expedition, with an Account of the Travels of Toussaint Charbonneau, and of Jean Baptiste, the Expedition Papoose* (Glendale, Calif.: Arthur H. Clark, 1933), 145-46.

6. David L. Bigler and Will Bagley, eds., *Army of Israel: Mormon Battalion Narratives* (Spokane, Wash.: Arthur H. Clark Company, 2000), IV, 145-46, n148; Bieber, 74.

7. Bieber, 74.

8. Bieber, 80-81; Ricketts, 9; Hebard, 146.

9. Daniel Tyler, *A Concise History of the Mormon Battalion in the Mexican War, 1846-1847* (1881; Reprint, Chicago: Rio Grande Press, 1964, 186-87, 188-89.

10. Bieber, 94-95.

11. Bieber, 94; Frank Alfred Golder, in collaboration with Thomas J. Bailey and Lyman Smith, eds.: *The March of the Mormon Battalion from Council Bluffs to California: Taken from the Journal of Henry Standage* (New York: Century Co., 1928), 182.

12. Bieber, 98, 100-101, 102, 104; Charles S. Peterson and others, *Mormon Battalion Trail Guide* (Salt Lake City: Utah State Historical Society, 1972); Forbes Parkhill, *The Blazed Trail of Antoine Leroux* (Los Angeles: Westernlore Press, 1965), 10-11, 207.

13. Bieber, 104.

14. Bieber, 105-7.

15. Bieber, 110-12: Ricketts, 86.

16. Bieber, 112.

17. Bieber, 113; Rebecca Jones, "The Journal of Nathaniel V. Jones, with the Mormon Battalion (extracted)," *Utah Historical Quarterly*, January, 1931, 7.

18. Bieber, 115-17.

19. Bieber, 124-25, 140.

20. Bieber, 145-46, 147; Bieber, 151-52; Ricketts, ix.

21. Bieber, 200-207.

22. Bieber, 171-72; Ricketts, x.

23. Bieber, 200-08.

24. Allan Nevins, *Frémont: Pathmarker of the West* (New York:

Longmans, Green, 1955), 227; Dale Morgan, ed., *Overland in 1846: Diaries and Letters of the California-Oregon Trail* (Georgetown, Calif.: Talisman Press, 1963), II, 654; Ricketts, 114.

25. Auguste Duhaut-Cilly, translated and edited by August Fruge' and Neal Harlow, *A Voyage to California, the Sandwich Islands and Around the World in the Years 1826-1829* (Berkeley: University of California Press, 1999), xi, 114.

26. Fr. Zephyrin Engelhardt, *San Luis Rey Mission* (San Francisco: James H. Barry Company, 1921), 156, 157-59.

27. Tyler, 187, 252-54, 264.

28. Bieber, 238-40.

29. Ricketts, 135-36.

Chapter Fourteen: John B. Charbonneau

1. Daniel Tyler, *A Concise History of the Mormon Battalion in the Mexican War, 1846-1847* (1881; reprint, Chicago: Rio Grande Press, 1964), 187-88, 256, 263, 265; Fr. Zephyrin Engelhardt, *San Luis Rey Mission* (San Francisco: James H. Barry Company, 1921), 145-47.

2. Robert G. Athearn, *William Tecumseh Sherman and the Settlement of the West* (Norman: University of Oklahoma Press, 1995), xi-xii; Irving W. Anderson, "J. B. Charbonneau, Son of Sacajawea," *Oregon Historical Quarterly*, September, 1970, 260; LeRoy R. Hafen, *The Mountain Men and the Fur Trade of the Far West: Biographical Sketches of the Participants by Scholars of the Subject* (Glendale, Calif.: Arthur H. Clark, 1965), I, 219-20; Chris Moore, "Sacajawea's Son's Long-Lost Grave May Be Rescued from Oblivion," Ontario, Oregon *Argus-Observer*, Feb. 10, 1966, Section 2; Tyler, 264.

3. Hafen, 219-20.

4. James P. Beckwourth, *The Life and Adventures of James P. Beckwourth as told to Thomas D. Bonner* (1856; Reprint, Lincoln: University of Nebraska Press, 1972), 507-509.

5. J. M. Letts, *California Illustrated, Including a Description of the Panama and Nicaragua Routes* (New York: R. T. Young, 1853), 92; John Francis McDermott, ed., "Gold Fever: The Letters of 'Solitaire,' Goldrush Correspondent of '49," *The Bulletin*, Missouri Historical Society, October, 1949, 34; Elinor Wilson, *Jim Beckwourth: Black Mountain Man and War Chief of*

the Crows (Norman: University of Oklahoma Press, 1972), 122-23; Bonner, 598; Wilson, 125-27; Norman McLeod, "Heritage: Jean Baptiste Charbonneau, Cultured Mountain Man," *Sierra Heritage,* undated clipping, 22; Clyde H. Porter, "Jean Baptiste Charbonneau," *Idaho Yesterdays,* Fall, 1961, 8.

6. Hafen, I, 221, quoting Prince Paul's Sacramento Journal, translated by Louis C. Butscher, University of Wyoming.

7. Anonymous, "Death of a California Pioneer," Auburn, California *Placer Herald,* July 7, 1866, p. 2, col. 3; U.S. Census California, 1860, 63; Hafen, I, 221-22; William B. Carr, "Auburn Seeks to Preserve Landmarks Threatened by New Businesses," *Sacramento Bee,* B-1, Feb. 15, 1959; Advertisement, "Orleans Hotel," *Placer Herald,* Jan. 19, 1861 (Photocopies from Auburn-Placer County Library).

8. Dorothy M. Johnson, *The Bloody Bozeman: The Perilous Trail to Montana's Gold* (New York: McGraw-Hill, 1971), 4-7, n339.

9. Henry Edgar, "Journal of Henry Edgar - 1863," *Contributions to the Historical Society of Montana,* 1900, 137; Peter Ronan, "Discovery of Alder Gulch," *Contributions to the Historical Society of Montana,* 1900, 148; Grace Raymond Hebard and E. A. Brininstool, *The Bozeman Trail* (Cleveland: Arthur H. Clark, 1922), 206; Johnson, 44-45, 51-52; Robert G. Athearn, ed. "From Illinois to Montana in 1866: The Diary of Perry A. Burgess," *Pacific Northwest Quarterly,* January, 1950, 43.

10. Brigham D. Madsen, *The Lemhi: Sacajawea's People* (Caldwell, Idaho: Caxton Printers, 1979), 42-43, 48, 52-53.

11. McLeod, 23; Anderson, *Charbonneau Family Portrait,* 18; Anonymous, "Died," Ruby City, Idaho, *Owyhee Avalanche,* June 2, 1866.

12. Anonymous, "Death of a California Pioneer," Auburn, California *Placer Herald,* July 7, 1866, p. 2, col. 3.

Epilogue

1. Grace Raymond Hebard, "Pilot of First White Men to Cross the American Continent," *Journal of American History: Relating Life Stories of Men and Events that Have Entered into the Building of the Western Continent* (New Haven, Conn.: Associated Publishers of American Records, 1907), vol. 1, no. 3, 467-484.

2. Russell Reid, "Sakakawea," *North Dakota History,* July, 1963, 109; Hebard, *Sacajawea: A Guide and Interpreter of the Lewis and Clark Expedition, with an Account of the Travels of Toussaint Charbonneau, and of Jean Baptiste, the Expedition Papoose* (Glendale, Calif.: Arthur H. Clark, 1933), 208; John F. Roberts, "Rev. John Roberts, Shoshone Missionary, Gives Indian Bureau His Story on Sacajawea's Burial," *Billings Gazette,* March 31, 1935, 1, 6.

3. Roberts, 1; Reid, 101; Hebard, "Pilot," 468.

4. Faculty of the University of Wyoming, In Memoriam: Grace Raymond Hebard, 1861-1936, June, 1937, Folder 3, Box H352, Hebard papers; "Death Claims Dr. Hebard; Funeral Set for Tuesday," *Laramie Republican-Boomerang,* Oct. 12, 1936.

5. Hebard, "Pilot," 468; Irving W. Anderson, *A Charbonneau Family Portrait* (Astoria, Ore.: Fort Clatsop Historical Association, 1992), 9.

6. Anderson, *Family Portrait,* 9-10.

7. "Letters Received, 1877, Wyoming, S-1126 (Enclosure), Records of the Office of Indian Affairs, Photocopy from National Archives; Census Roll of the Shoshone Tribe of Indians Present at the Shoshone and Bannock Agency, Wyoming Territory, November 1, 1877, with letter of transmittal from James I. Patten, Indian agent, Folder 2, B-SA14, Hebard papers.

8. Reuben Gold Thwaites, ed., *Early Western Travels,* VI, 32-33; Anderson, *Family Portrait,* 9.

9. Hebard, "Pilot," 479.

10. Helen Addison Porter, "The Mystery of Sacagawea's Death," *Pacific Northwest Quarterly,* Winter, 1964, 5; Irving W. Anderson, "Probing the Riddle of the Bird Woman," *Montana, the Magazine of Western History,* Autumn, 1973, 16 (with photocopy of Clark's account book entry from document in Newberry Library, Chicago); Anderson, *Family Portrait,* 10.

11. Hebard, *Sacajawea,* 216.

12. Anderson, "Probing the Riddle of the Bird Woman," *Montana, the Magazine of Western History,* Autumn, 1973, 16.

13. Anderson, *Family Portrait,* 10.

14. U. S. Census, California, 1863; Anonymous, "Death of a California Pioneer," Auburn, California *Placer Herald,* July 7, 1866, p. 2,

col. 3; Anonymous, "Died," Ruby City, Idaho, *Owyhee Avalanche*, June 2, 1866.

15. Hebard, *Sacajawea*, 147-48.

16. James K. Hosmer, *History of the Expedition of Lewis and Clark, 1804-1805* (Chicago: A. C. McClurg and Company, 1902), I, 408; Elliott Coues, ed. *History of the Expedition under the Command of Lewis and Clark* (New York: Francis P. Harper, 1893), II, 510; Nicholas Biddle, *History of the Expedition under the Command of Captains Lewis and Clark: A Complete Reprint of the Biddle Edition of 1814, to which all Members of the Expedition Contributed* (New York: Allerton Book Co., 1972), II, 74; Hebard, "Sacagawea and the Lewis and Clark Expedition," undated outline in Folder 1, Box SA-14, Hebard Papers; Thwaites, *Original Journals of the Lewis and Clark Expedition, 1804-1806* (New York: Dodd, Mead, 1904), II, Part Two, 361; Moulton, V, 109-15, XI, 283-85.

17. James Truslow Adams, "The Six Most Important American Women," *Good Housekeeping Magazine*, February, 1941, 30; The Associated Press, "Enzi Wants Image of Sacajawea on Coin," *Laramie Daily Boomerang*, July 12, 1998), 10.

18. Hebard, *Sacajawea*, 211.

19. Ibid.

20. William James, The Will to Believe, 1897. Quoted in R. W. B. Lewis, *The Jameses: A Family Narrative* (New York: Farrar, Straus and Giroux, 1991), 492.

21. Prologue to Laurence Olivier's film production of Shakespeare's *King Richard III*.

Bibliography

Archives and Manuscript Sources

Butscher, Louis C. *A Brief Biography of Prince Paul Wilhelm of Wurttemberg*. Laramie, Wyo.: 1930. Box 51, Folder 11, Grace Hebard Papers.

Hebard, Grace Raymond. Papers, 1829-1947, Accession Number 40008, American Heritage Center, University of Wyoming.

Government Publications

American State Papers, Class II, *Indian Affairs*, Volume II: *Accounts of Superintendents of Indian Affairs, 1822*. Washington, 1834. Typed copy in Grace Raymond Hebard Papers, 1829-1947, Accession Number 40008, Box Number 23, Folder Number 3, American Heritage Center, University of Wyoming.

Debates and Proceedings in the Congress of the United States, Ninth Congress, Second Session. Washington, D.C.: Gales and Seaton, 1852.

Hewitt, J. B. N., ed. *The Journal of Rudolph Friederich Kurz: The Life and Work of This Swiss Artist*. Bureau of American Ethnology Bulletin 115, Smithsonian Institution, Government Printing Office, Washington, D.C., 1937. Reprint, Fairfield: Ye Galleon Press, n.d.

Kappler, Charles J., ed. *Indian Affairs. Laws and Treaties*. 7 vols. Washington, D.C.: Government Printing Office, 1904.

Records of the Office of Indian Affairs, "Census Roll of the Shoshone Tribe of Indians, Present at the Shoshone and Bannock Agency, Wyoming Territory, Nov. 1, 1877."

U.S. Census California, 1860, Page 63.

Books

Abel, Annie Heloise, ed. *Chardon's Journal at Fort Clark, 1834-1839*. Pierre: Department of History, State of South Dakota, 1932.

_____. *Tabeau's Narrative of Loisel's Expedition to the Upper Missouri*. Norman: University of Oklahoma Press, 1939.

Allen, John Logan. *Passage through the Garden: Lewis and Clark and the Image of the American Northwest*. Urbana: University of Illinois Press, 1975.

Ambrose, Stephen E. *Undaunted Courage: Meriwether Lewis, Thomas Jefferson, and the Opening of the American West*. New York: Simon & Schuster, 1996.

Anderson, Irving W. *A Charbonneau Family Portrait: Biographical Sketches of Sacagawea, Jean Baptiste, and Toussaint Charbonneau*. Astoria, Ore.: Fort Clatsop Historical Association, 1992.

Athearn, Robert G. *William Tecumseh Sherman and the Settlement of the West*. Norman: University of Oklahoma Press, 1956, reprint 1995.

Bakeless, John. *Lewis & Clark: Partners in Discovery*. New York: W. Morrow, 1947.

Barness, Larry. *Gold Camp*. New York: Hastings House, 1963.

Bartlett, John Russell. *Personal Narrative of Explorations and Incidents in Texas, New Mexico, California, Sonora and Chihuahua Connected with the United States and Mexican Boundary Commission during the years 1850, '51, '52, and '53*. New York: D. Appleton, 1856.

Beckwourth, James P. *The Life and Times of James P. Beckwourth as told to Thomas D. Bonner*.
    1856. Reprint, Lincoln: University of Nebraska Press. 1972.

Biddle, Nicholas. *History of the Expedition under the Command of Captains Lewis and Clarke: A Complete Reprint of the Biddle Edition of 1814, to which all Members of the Expedition Contributed*, 3 vols. New York: Allerton Book Co., 1972.

Bieber, Ralph B., in collaboration with Averam B. Bender. *Exploring Southwestern Trails, 1846-1854, Vol. VII of The Southwest Historical Series*. Glendale, Calif.: Arthur H. Clark, 1938.

Bigler, David L., and Will Bagley, eds. *Army of Israel: Mormon Battalion Narratives*. Spokane, Wash.: Arthur H. Clark, 2000.

Chittenden, Hiram Martin. *The American Fur Trade of the West: A History of the Pioneer Trading Posts and Early Fur Companies of the Missouri Valley and the Rocky Mountains, and of the Overland Commerce with Santa Fe.* New York: F.P. Harper, 1902.

_____. *Fur Trade of the Far West.* Lincoln: University of Nebraska Press, 1986.

_____. *History of Early Steamboat Navigation on the Missouri River: Life and Adventures of Joseph LaBarge, Pioneer Navigator and Indian Trader.* New York: Francis P. Harper, 1903.

Chuinard, Eldon G. *Only One Man Died: The Medical Aspects of the Lewis and Clark Expedition.* Glendale, Calif.: Arthur H. Clark, 1979.

Clark, Ella E., and Margot Edmonds. *Sacagawea of the Lewis and Clark Expedition.* Berkeley: University of California Press, 1979.

Clarke, Charles G. *The Men of the Lewis and Clark Expedition: A Biographical Roster of the Fifty-One Members and a Composite Diary of Their Activities from All Known Sources.* Glendale, Calif.: Arthur H. Clark, 1970.

Cooke, P. St. George. *The Conquest of New Mexico and California: An Historical and Personal Narrative.* New York: G. P. Putnam's Sons, 1878.

Coues, Elliott, ed. *History of the Expedition under the Command of Lewis and Clark.* 4 vols. New York: Francis P. Harper, 1893. Reprint, Dodd Mead, 1904, 3 vols.

_____, ed. *New Light on the Early History of the Greater Northwest: The Manuscript Journals of Alexander Henry, Fur Trader of the Northwest Company, and of David Thompson, Official Geographer and Explorer of the Same Company.* 3 vols. New York: Francis P. Harper, 1897.

DeVoto, Bernard. *Across the Wide Missouri.* Boston: Houghton Mifflin, 1947.

_____. *The Course of Empire.* Boston: Houghton Mifflin, 1952.

_____, ed. *The Journals of Lewis and Clark.* Boston: Houghton Mifflin, 1953.

Duhaut-Cilly, Auguste, translated and edited by August Fruge' and Neal Harlow. *A Voyage to California, the Sandwich Islands and Around the World in the Years 1826-1829.* Berkeley: University of California Press, 1999.

Duncan, Dayton. *Out West: An American Journey.* New York: Viking, 1987.

Egan, Ferol. *Frémont: Explorer for a Restless Nation.* Reno: University of Nevada Press, 1985.

Engelhardt, Fr. Zephyrin. *San Luis Rey Mission.* San Francisco: James H. Barry Company, 1921.

Ewers, John C., et al. *Views of a Vanishing Frontier.* Omaha: Center for Western Studies/ Joslyn Art Museum, 1984.

Ferris, Warren Angus. *Life in the Rocky Mountains, 1830-1835.* Salt Lake City: Rocky Mountain Book Shop, 1940.

Foley, William E., and C. David Rice. *The First Chouteaus: River Barons of Early St. Louis.* Urbana: University of Illinois Press, 1983.

Forrest, Earle R. *Patrick Gass: Lewis and Clark's Last Man.* Independence: Mrs. A.M. Painter, 1950.

Frémont, John Charles. *The Life of Col. John Charles Frémont and His Narratives of Explorations and Adventures in Kansas, Nebraska, Oregon and California.* New York: Miller, Orton and Mulligan, 1856.

_____. *Memoirs of My Life.* Chicago: Belford, Clarke, 1887.

Golder, Frank Alfred, in collaboration with Thomas J. Bailey and Lyman Smith, eds. *The March of the Mormon Battalion from Council Bluffs to California: Taken from the Journal of Henry Standage.* New York: Century, 1928.

Hafen, LeRoy R., ed. *The Mountain Men and the Fur Trade of the Far West: Biographical Sketches of the Participants by Scholars of the Subject.* Glendale, Calif.: Arthur H. Clark Company, 1965.

_____ and Ann W. Hafen, eds., *To the Rockies and Oregon, 1839-1842.* Glendale, Calif.: Arthur H. Clark, 1955.

_____ and Francis Marion Young. *Fort Laramie and the Pageant of the West, 1834-1890.* Glendale, Calif.: Arthur H. Clark, 1938.

Haines, Aubrey L., ed. *Osborne Russell's Journal of a Trapper.* Portland: Oregon Historical Society, 1955; Reprint, Lincoln: University of Nebraska Press, 1967.

Hamilton, Ladd. *Snowbound.* Pullman: Washington State University Press, 1997.

Hebard, Grace Raymond. *Sacajawea: A Guide and Interpreter of the Lewis and Clark Expedition, with an Account of the Travels of Toussaint Charbonneau, and of Jean Baptiste, the Expedition Papoose.* Glendale, Calif.: Arthur H. Clark, 1933.

_____ and E. A. Brininstool. *The Bozeman Trail.* Cleveland: Arthur H. Clark,

1922.

Heizer, Robert F., ed. *California*. Vol. 8 of *Handbook of North American Indians*, Washington: Smithsonian Institution, 1978.

Hollon, W. Eugene. *The Lost Pathfinder: Zebulon Montgomery Pike*. Norman: University of Oklahoma Press, 1949.

Holmberg, James J., ed. *Dear Brother: Letters of William Clark to Jonathan Clark*. New Haven: Yale University Press, 2002.

Hosmer, James Kendall. *History of the Expedition of Lewis and Clark, 1804-1805*. Chicago: A. C. McClurg, 1902.

_____, ed. *Gass's Journal of the Lewis and Clark Expedition*. Chicago: A. C. McClurg, 1904.

Jackson, Donald, ed. *Letters of the Lewis and Clark Expedition with Related Documents, 1783-1854*, 2d ed. 2 vols. Urbana: University of Illinois Press, 1978.

James, Thomas. *Three Years among the Indians and Mexicans*. Edited by Walter P. Douglas. St. Louis: Missouri Historical Society, 1916.

Johnson, Dorothy M. *The Bloody Bozeman: The Perilous Trail to Montana's Gold*. New York: McGraw-Hill, 1971.

Kennerly, William Clark, as told to Elizabeth Russell. *Persimmon Hill: A Narrative of Old St. Louis and the Far West*. Norman: University of Oklahoma Press, 1949.

Kessler, Donna J. *The Making of Sacagawea: A Euro-American Legend*. Tuscaloosa: University of Alabama Press, 1996.

Larpenteur, Charles. *Forty Years a Fur Trader on the Upper Missouri*. Lincoln: University of Nebraska Press, 1989.

Lavender, David. *Bent's Fort*. Garden City, N.Y.: Doubleday, 1954.

Letts, J. M. *California Illustrated, Including a Description of the Panama and Nicaragua Routes*. New York: R. T. Young, 1853.

Lewis, Meriwether and Clark, William. *The Journals of the Lewis & Clark Expedition*. 13 vols. Edited by Gary E. Moulton. Lincoln: University of Nebraska Press, 1983-2001.

Luttig, John C. *Journal of a Fur-trading Expedition on the Missouri River, 1812-1813*. Edited by Stella M. Drumm. 1920; Reprint, New York: Argosy-Antiquarian Press, 1964.

MacGregor, Carol Lynn, ed. *The Journals of Patrick Gass: Member of the*

Lewis and Clark Expedition. Missoula: Mountain Press Publishing Company, 1997.

Madsen, Brigham D. *The Lemhi: Sacajawea's People.* Caldwell, Idaho: Caxton Printers, 1979.

Malone, Dumas. *Jefferson and His Time.* Boston: Little, Brown, 1948-1981.

Meriwether, David. *My Life in the Mountains and on the Plains: The Newly Discovered Autobiography.* Edited by Robert A. Griffen. Norman: University of Oklahoma Press, 1965.

Meyer, Roy W. *The Village Indians of the Upper Missouri: The Mandans, Hidatsas, and Arikaras.* Lincoln: University of Nebraska Press, 1977.

Morgan, Dale, ed. *Overland in 1846: Diaries and Letters of the California-Oregon Trail.* 2 vols. Georgetown: Talisman Press, 1963.

_____. *The West of William H. Ashley: The international struggle for the fur trade of the Missouri, the Rocky Mountains, and the Columbia, with explorations beyond the Continental Divide, recorded in the diaries and letters of William H. Ashley and his contemporaries, 1822-1838.* Denver: Old West Publishing Company, 1964.

Nasatir, A.P., ed. *Before Lewis and Clark: Documents Illustrating the History of the Missouri, 1785-1804.* 2 vols. St. Louis: St. Louis Historical Documents Foundation, 1952.

Nevins, Allan. *Frémont: Pathmarker of the West.* New York: Longmans, Green, 1955.

Newman, Peter C. *Company of Adventurers: The Story of the Hudson's Bay Company.* 2 vols. Harmondsworth, Middlesex, England: Penguin Books, 1985.

Oglesby, Richard Edward. *Manuel Lisa and the Opening of the Missouri Fur Trade.* Norman: University of Oklahoma Press, 1963.

Olmsted, Gerald W. *Fielding's Lewis & Clark Trail.* New York: William Morrow, 1986.

Osgood, Ernest Staples, ed. *The Field Notes of Captain William Clark, 1803-1805.* New Haven: Yale University Press, 1964.

Parkhill, Forbes. *The Blazed Trail of Antoine Leroux.* Los Angeles: Westernlore Press, 1965.

Peterson, Charles S. and others, *Mormon Battalion Trail Guide.* Salt Lake City: Utah State Historical Society, 1972.

Porter, Mae Reed, and Odessa Davenport. *Scotsman in Buckskin: Sir William Drummond Stewart and the Rocky Mountain Fur Trade*. New York: Hastings House, 1963.

Quaife, Milo M., ed. *The Journals of Captain Meriwether Lewis and Sergeant John Ordway*. Madison: State Historical Society of Wisconsin, 1916.

Ricketts, Norma Baldwin. *The Mormon Battalion: U.S. Army of the West, 1846-1848*. Logan: Utah State University Press, 1996.

Robinson, Elwyn B. *History of North Dakota*. Lincoln: University of Nebraska Press, 1966.

Rollins, Philip Ashton, ed. *The Discovery of the Oregon Trail: Robert Stuart's Narratives of His Overland Trip Eastward from Astoria in 1812-13*. Lincoln: University of Nebraska Press, 1995.

Ronda, James P. *Lewis and Clark among the Indians*. Lincoln: University of Nebraska Press, 1984.

Ruxton, George Frederic. *In the Old West: As It Was in the Days of Kit Carson and the "Mountain Men."* Cleveland: International Fiction Library, 1915.

_____. *Life in the Far West*. New York: Harper & Brothers, 1849.

Sage, Rufus B. *Rocky Mountain Life or, Startling Scenes and Perilous Adventures in the Far West during an Expedition of Three Years*. Boston: Wentworth, 1858. Reprint, Lincoln: University of Nebraska Press, 1982.

Schultz, James Willard. *Bird Woman (Sacajawea) The Guide of Lewis and Clark*. Boston: Houghton Mifflin, 1918.

Skarsten, M. O. *George Drouillard: Hunter and Interpreter for Lewis and Clark and Fur Trader, 1807-1810*. Glendale, Calif.: Arthur H. Clark, 1964.

Stuart, Granville. *Forty Years on the Frontier*. 2 vols. in one. Glendale, Calif.: Arthur H. Clark, 1957.

Sunder, John E. *Joshua Pilcher: Fur Trader and Indian Agent*. Norman: University of Oklahoma Press, 1968.

Terrell, John Upton. *Black Robe: The Life of Pierre-Jean De Smet, Missionary, Explorer & Pioneer*. Garden City, N.Y., Doubleday, 1964.

_____. *Furs by Astor*. New York: William Morrow, 1963.

Thompson, Erwin N. *Fort Union Trading Post: Fur Trade Empire on the Upper Missouri*. Williston, N.Dak.: Fort Union Association, 1994.

Thwaites, Reuben Gold, ed. *Early Western Travels, 1748-1846.* 32 vols. Cleveland: Arthur H. Clark, 1904, et seq.

_____. *Original Journals of the Lewis and Clark Expedition, 1804-1806.* New York: Dodd, Mead, 1904.

Tyler, Daniel. *A Concise History of the Mormon Battalion in the Mexican War, 1846-1847.* 1881. Reprint, Chicago: Rio Grande Press, 1964.

Van Kirk, Sylvia. *Many Tender Ties: Women in Fur-Trade Society, 1670-1870.* Norman: University of Oklahoma Press, 1980.

Vestal, Stanley. *Kit Carson: The Happy Warrior of the Old West.* Boston: Houghton Mifflin, 1931.

West, Elliott. *The Way to the West: Essays on the Central Plains.* Albuquerque: University of New Mexico Press, 1995.

Wheeler, Olin D. *The Trail of Lewis and Clark, 1804, 1904.* 2 vols. New York: G. P. Putnam's Sons, 1904.

Wilson, Elinor. *Jim Beckwourth: Black Mountain Man and War Chief of the Crows.* Norman: University of Oklahoma Press, 1972.

Wolle, Muriel V. S. *Montana Pay Dirt.* Denver: Sage Books, 1963.

Wood, W. Raymond and Margot Liberty, eds. *Anthropology on the Great Plains.* Lincoln: University of Nebraska Press, 1980.

Wood, W. Raymond and Thomas D. Thiessen, eds. *Early Fur Trade on the Northern Plains.* Norman: University of Oklahoma Press, 1985.

Articles

Adams, James Truslow. "The Six Most Important American Women." *Good Housekeeping Magazine,* February, 1941.

Advertisement, "Orleans Hotel." Auburn, California *Placer Herald,* Jan. 19, 1861.

Anderson, Irving W. "Fort Manuel: Its Historical Significance." *South Dakota History,* Spring, 1976.

_____. "J. B. Charbonneau, Son of Sacajawea." *Oregon Historical Quarterly,* September, 1970.

_____. "Letter to the Editor: J. B. Charbonneau, to Date." *Oregon Historical Quarterly,* March, 1971.

_____. "Probing the Riddle of the Bird Woman." *Montana, the Magazine of Western History,* Autumn, 1973.

_____. "Sacajawea, Sacagawea, Sakakawea?" *South Dakota History*, Fall, 1978.

Anderson, Irving W., and Blanche Schroer. "Sacagawea: Her Name and Her Destiny." *We Proceeded On*, November, 1999.

Anonymous. "Death Claims Dr. Hebard; Funeral Set for Tuesday." *Laramie Republican-Boomerang*, October 12, 1936.

Anonymous. "Death of a California Pioneer." Auburn, California *Placer-Herald*, July 7, 1866.

_____. "Died." Ruby City, Idaho *Owyhee Avalanche*. June 2, 1866.

Associated Press. "Enzi Wants Image of Sacagawea on Coin." *Laramie Daily Boomerang*, July 12, 1998.

Athearn, Robert G. ed., "From Illinois to Montana in 1866: The Diary of Perry A. Burgess." *Pacific Northwest Quarterly*, January, 1950.

Barry, J. Neilson. "Journal of E. Willard Smith while with the Fur Traders Vasquez and Sublette, in the Rocky Mountain Region, 1839-1840." *Quarterly of the Oregon Historical Society*, March, 1913.

Barry, Louise, ed. "William Clark's Diary, May, 1826-February, 1831: Part One." *Kansas Historical Quarterly*, February, 1948.

Beaty, Hilde. "Louis and Toussaint Charbonneau." *Families*, February, 1987.

Beauregard, Mrs. H. T., translator, "Journal of Jean Baptiste Trudeau among the Arikara Indians in 1795." *Missouri Historical Society Collections*, 1912-1923.

Berquist, Alvera. "Karl Bodmer." *We Proceeded On*, May, 1999.

Butscher, Louis C. "A Brief Biography of Prince Paul Wilhelm of Wurttemberg (1797-1860)." *New Mexico Historical Review*, July, 1942.

Carr, William C. "Auburn Seeks to Preserve Landmarks Threatened by New Businesses." *Sacramento Bee*, B- 1, Feb. 15, 1959.

Cleary, Rita. "Charbonneau Reconsidered." *We Proceeded On*, May, 2000.

Crawford, Helen, "Sakakawea." *North Dakota Historical Quarterly*, April, 1927.

Creel, George. "Path of Empire." *Collier's*, April 17, 1926.

Cruikshank, Ernest Alexander. "Robert Dickson, the Indian Trader." *Collections of the State Historical Society of Wisconsin*, 1892.

Cutright, Paul Russell. "I Gave Him Barks and Saltpeter." *American Heritage*, December, 1963.

Dale, Harrison C., ed. "A Fragmentary Journal of William L. Sublette." *Mississippi Valley Historical Review*, June, 1919.

Duncan, Dayton. "Lewis and Clark's Old Glory." *We Proceeded On*, November, 1999.

Dunn, Adrian R. "A History of Old Fort Berthold." *North Dakota History*, October, 1963.

Edgar, Henry. "Journal of Henry Edgar-1863." *Contributions to the Historical Society of Montana*, 1900.

Gibbons, Loren M., "All Them Horses and One Poor Mule." *We Proceeded On*, August, 2002.

Hebard, Grace Raymond. "Pilot of First White Men to Cross the American Continent." *Journal of American History: Relating Life Stories of Men and Events that Have Entered into the Building of the Western Continent*. New Haven, Conn., vol. 1, no. 3, 1907.

Howard, Helen Addison. "The Mystery of Sacagawea's Death." *Pacific Northwest Quarterly*, January, 1967.

Hunt, Robert. "Crime and Punishment on the Lewis and Clark Expedition." *We Proceeded On*, May and August, 1989.

_____. "Luck or Providence? Narrow Escapes on the Lewis and Clark Expedition." *We Proceeded On*, August, 1999.

Jones, Rebecca M. "The Journal of Nathaniel V. Jones, with the Mormon Battalion (extracted)." *Utah Historical Quarterly*, January, 1931.

Kirkpatrick, Glen. "The Rediscovery of Clark's Point of View." *We Proceeded On*, February, 1999.

McDermott, John Francis, ed. "Gold Fever: The Letters of 'Solitaire,' Goldrush Correspondent of '49." *The Bulletin*, Missouri Historical Society, October, 1949.

McLeod, Norman. "Heritage: Jean Baptiste Charbonneau, Cultured Mountain Man." *Sierra Heritage*, undated clipping.

Moore, Bob. "A Closer Look at the Uniforms of the Lewis and Clark Expedition." *We Proceeded On*, November, 1998.

_____. "Pompey's Baptism." *We Proceeded On*, February, 2000.

Moore, Chris. "Sacajawea's Son's Long-Lost Grave May Be Rescued from Oblivion." Ontario, OR *Argus-Observer*, Feb. 10, 1966.

Nicholson, Blake. "Sacagawea or Sakakawea: Debate over Indian woman's name goes another round." *Santa Fe New Mexican*, October 29, 2002.

_____. "'Sakakawea' spelling change considered by tribes council." *Casper Star-Tribune*, August 16, 2002

Nute, Grace Lee. "James Dickson: A Filibuster in Minnesota in 1836." *Mississippi Valley Historical Review*, September, 1923.

Olson, James C. ed. "From Nebraska City to Montana, 1866; The Diary of Thomas Alfred Creigh." *Nebraska History*, September, 1948.

Ottoson, Dennis R. "Toussaint Charbonneau: A Most Durable Man." *South Dakota History*, Spring, 1976.

Peebles, John J. "Rugged Waters: Trails and Campsites of Lewis and Clark in the Salmon River Country." *Idaho Yesterdays*, Summer, 1964.

Porter, Clyde H. "Jean Baptiste Charbonneau." *Idaho Yesterdays*, Fall, 1961.

Reid, Russell. "Sakakawea." *North Dakota History*, July, 1963.

_____ and Clell G. Gannon, eds., "Journal of the Atkinson-O'Fallon Expedition." *North Dakota Historical Quarterly*, October, 1929.

Roberts, John. "Rev. John Roberts, Shoshone Missionary, Gives Indian Bureau His Story on Sacajawea's Burial." *Billings Gazette*, March 31, 1935, 1,6.

Robinson, Doane. "A Sioux Indian View of the Last War with England." *South Dakota Historical Collections*, 1910.

_____. "South Dakota and the War of 1812." *South Dakota Historical Collections*, 1924.

Ronan, Peter. "Discovery of Alder Gulch." *Contributions to the Historical Society of Montana*, 1900.

Saindon, Bob. "The Abduction of Sacagawea." *We Proceeded On*, Spring, 1976.

Schroer, Blanche. "Sacajawea: The Legend and the Truth." *In Wyoming*, December-January, 1978.

Stevens, O. A. "Maximilian in North Dakota, 1833-34." *North Dakota History*, 1961.

Stewart, Frank H. "Mandan and Hidatsa Villages in the Eighteenth and Nineteenth Centuries." *Plains Anthropology*, November, 1974.

Taber, Ronald W. "Sacagawea and the Suffragettes: An Interpretation of a Myth." *Pacific Northwest Quarterly*, January, 1967.

Thom, James Alexander. "Life among the Nee Mee Poo." *We Proceeded On*, May, 2000.

Truax, Allen L. "Fort Mandan, 1804-06." *North Dakota Historical Quarterly*, October, 1927.

_____. "Manuel Lisa and His North Dakota Trading Post." *North Dakota Historical Quarterly*, July, 1928.

Trudeau, Jean Baptiste. "Trudeau's Journal." *South Dakota Historical Collections*, 1914.

Weisbrod, Marie Webster. "One Remarkable Lady: An Interview with Blanche Schroer." *We Proceeded On*, February, 1998.

Wilhelm, Paul, Duke of Wurttemberg. "First Journey to North America in the Years 1822 to 1824." Translated by William G. Bek. *South Dakota History Collections*, 1938.

Young, F. G., ed. N. J. Wyeth's "Correspondence and Journals." *Sources of the History of Oregon*, I.

Index

Index